WAITING
FOR THE
SECOND
COMING

Discovery House
PUBLISHERS
BOX 3566 · GRAND RAPIDS. MI 49501

PUBLISHING BOOKS THAT FEED
THE SOUL WITH THE WORD OF GOD.

WAITING
FOR THE
SECOND
COMING

*Studies in
Thessalonians*

RAY C. STEDMAN

Waiting for the Second Coming
Copyright © 1990 by Ray C. Stedman

Unless indicated otherwise, Scripture is taken from the
HOLY BIBLE, NEW INTERNATIONAL VERSION.
Copyright © 1973, 1978, 1984 International Bible Society.
Used by permission of Zondervan Bible Publishers.

Library of Congress Cataloging-in-Publication-Data

Stedman, Ray C.
    Waiting for the second coming : studies in Thessalonians /
Ray C. Stedman.
        p.   cm.
    ISBN: 0-929239-14-8

    1. Bible. N.T. Thessalonians—Criticism, interpretation, etc.
I. Title.
BS2725.2.S74 1989
227'.8106—dc20   89-16936
                                                        CIP

Discovery House Publishers is affiliated with
RBC Ministries, Grand Rapids, Michigan 49512

Discovery House books are distributed to the trade exclusively by
Barbour Publishing, Inc., Uhrichsville, Ohio 44683

Printed in the United States of America

06 07 08 09 10 / CHG / 15 14 13 12 11 10 9 8

CONTENTS

PREFACE

MARTIN LUTHER once said: "My hope despairs; but my despair keeps me hoping!" A similar philosophy seems to govern the masses of men and women today. It is a spreading miasma that has even seeped into the hearts of many Christians who evidence it by giving up once-held moral standards, who look for more and more governmental subsidies to replace honest earnings. While the world grows hard and cold to spiritual matters, church members feel a loss of personal faith and find their churches less and less relevant to the issues of modern life.

These same threatening clouds gathered about the young church at Thessalonica in the fifth decade of the first century—that body of believers which the apostle Paul and his companions had seen spring into vigorous faith but two short years before. In response, Paul wrote two letters to the Thessalonians, and the help he gave them is exactly what many Christians need today to help them live amid the pressures of our times.

The Thessalonians needed a father's faithful concern; a mother's tender, understanding words; a brother's readiness to stand by to the end; and, above all, a realization of the resources they already possessed in the Spirit's inner strengthening. They needed to realize anew that the dark powers they faced were being kept within rigid limits and that relief was certain to come in God's time from their returning Lord.

These two letters speak as clearly and powerfully in the late twentieth century as they did in the first. Let us read them as eagerly and avidly as Paul's converts must have read them fresh from his pen.

1
THESSALONIANS

CHANGED LIVES 1
(1:1–10)

*T*HE THESSALONIAN letters of the apostle Paul were written to a young church struggling to survive in an extremely dangerous world. Within twenty years of their writing, the whole of the ancient East was convulsed in warfare and rebellion. In A.D. 70 the armies of Titus surrounded Jerusalem. Following a bloody siege the city was overrun, the temple destroyed, and the Jews taken captive. The movements that culminated in these events had already begun when this first letter was written. Thus it is clear that the Thessalonian Christians were facing perilous times.

We too are living in dangerous times. Many years ago, Dr. E. M. Blaiklock, who was then Professor of Classics at the University of Auckland in New Zealand, said something I have never forgotten. This renowned biblical historian declared: "Of all the centuries, the twentieth is most like the first." We can, therefore, feel very close to this young church in Thessalonica.

Many today sense an approaching world crisis. A nervous, jittery stock market; a growing sense of cynicism and distrust of the political process; an increase in drug and alcohol dependency, with the resultant physical and mental toll in human lives; scientists tinkering with our genetic make-up and actually developing a business of selling fetal tissues; all these portend a frightening crisis looming on the horizon of our times. Add to this the now familiar threat of AIDS, the spread of famine in many countries, and, of course, the ever-present threat of nuclear warfare, and it is clear that something terrible is about to happen. We are living in a world in chaos.

Back in 1980 leaders from all over the Western world attended the First Global Conference on the Future, held in Ontario, Canada. The chairman of that conference spoke these sobering words: "The bad news is that the end of the world is coming. The good news is, not yet. But the decade of the 1980s is going to be the most important in human history. If we don't make the right decisions, the odds of our going beyond this decade are very slim. The danger of war and the collapse of Western civilization is a very real possibility."

Even earlier, in 1972, a group of international industrial leaders and thinkers, called the Club of Rome, suggested six proposals that humanity must put into effect if we are to survive on this planet. I will share only the first, but very significant, proposal: "The survival of this planet necessitates new forms of thinking that will lead to a fundamental revision of human behavior and, by implication, of the entire fabric of present-day society." That simply says that if we cannot discover how to change people, there is no hope of saving the world from ultimate collapse. In the immortal words of Pogo, "We has met the enemy, and he is us." There is no way out unless society can find a means of fundamentally changing human beings.

Right here is the glory of our message, for the gospel changes men and women. Paul wrote letters to the young church at Thessalonica because people there had found in the good news about Jesus a way to be changed. The focus and purpose of their lives had been drastically altered.

Paul himself founded this church in Salonica (as it is now called). It is today a bustling center of northern Greece, one of the few New Testament cities that is still flourishing. The ancient gate through which the apostle entered the city spanned the Egnatian Way, the Roman road that ran from the Adriatic to the Bosphorus. After Paul and his friends had been treated shamefully in Philippi, they journeyed on about 100 miles west to Thessalonica. Paul remained there at least three weeks and probably longer, but he was able to minister in the synagogue for only three sabbaths.

The Jews of the city became so enraged by his teaching about Jesus that they created a riot and captured Paul's host, Jason, holding him responsible for the apostle's behavior. Paul left the city, traveling south to Berea and there began to preach again. The Jews from Thessalonica, however, followed him, causing another uprising in Berea. Finally, Paul was sent on alone to Athens. He remained there a short time and then moved to Corinth. It was from that city, in A.D. 50 or 51, that he addressed this letter to the Thessalonian believers, only a few weeks old in Christ.

A DUAL ADDRESS

In the salutation Paul gives a double address for the church: one, geographical, the other, spiritual. The new believers lived in Thessalonica, but they were also found "in God the Father and the Lord Jesus Christ" (1:1). Of the two addresses, the latter is the more important. If we have come to Christ, we must see ourselves as primarily new creatures "in God the Father " and "in the Lord Jesus Christ."

Paul is continually thankful in prayer for three things these believers possess: their faith, their love, and their hope. In the New Testament, these are always listed as fundamental characteristics of those who have come to Christ. At the close of that wonderful thirteenth chapter of 1 Corinthians, Paul says: "And now these three remain: faith, hope and love. But the greatest of these is love" (13:13). And, he reminds us, these three qualities will never end.

In reading Paul's letters I never tire of noting how his mind works. He has a marvelous ability to summarize many points in a single verse and then amplify them again in easy-to-follow steps. As we see in these early verses, Paul is not speaking of mere faith, hope, and love. He is very careful to be specific—a faith *that works*, a love *that labors*, and a hope *that endures*—the great motives of the Christian life. If you have true faith, if you have love born of the Spirit, and if you have hope in the coming of Christ, you will be motivated to live as you ought today.

THE WORK OF FAITH

What is this "work of faith" that Paul mentions? He sums it up himself in verse 9. There he recognizes that the Thessalonians had "turned to God from idols to serve the living and true God." That is faith at work. Faith is not merely belief; faith works. It has the power to change. Faith enables you to turn from what is wrong to what is right, from dark and hurtful things to right and true and healthy things, from the worship of idols to the worship of God.

Notice the direction of this action: *to* God *from* idols, not the other way around. You do not leave your idols for some reason and then painfully try to find God. What happens is that you discover something of the beauty, the glory, and the greatness of God; and, seeing that and wanting it, you are willing to forsake the cheap and tawdry things you once believed could satisfy.

Modern America is surely one of the most idolatrous countries the world has ever seen. We are surrounded with idol worship. I once heard of a Chinese man who visited here and was asked upon his return to China whether Americans worshiped idols. "Yes, they do," he reported. "They have three of them. In the winter they worship a fat man in a red suit. In the spring they worship a rabbit. And in the fall they sacrifice a turkey!" Although there may be a shade of truth to this clever line, these are not true idols; for the most part they are myths and legends we pass along to each generation.

Television might properly be labeled an idol. Too many spend far too long glued to that staring eye, which feeds all types of ideas and emotions into their minds. But I don't think that television is really an idol. It is, rather, an altar upon which we spread offerings and sacrifices to the great god of Self. Television panders to our lust for comfort and entertainment. It lures us to think always of our own comfort, our pleasure, our fear of boredom, our desire to be either thrilled or terrified by watching some spectacle or event. It encourages us to focus on ourselves. But Self is the true idol.

The Habits of the Heart, a book written by a group of contemporary psychologists, develops the thesis that television causes Americans to forget how to serve. Perhaps this is not nearly as evident in Christian circles as it is in the world at large, but we face it also in the body of Christ. Jesus said that He came "not to be ministered unto, but to minister and to give himself." This is the source of true richness and fulfillment. When we demand to be ministered to, when we must always have something titillating our senses, the end is loneliness, emptiness, and ultimately despair. The proof is visible everywhere today.

America obviously also worships Eros, the goddess of sex, and Baal, the erotic deity associated with fertility rites. Baal worship in the ancient world promoted degenerate practices of the most licentious kind and is behind many of the loathsome practices in our country today. Baal worship is manifested in the rise of homosexuality as an acceptable life-style. It is behind the pornography that pervades almost every aspect of modern life. More than that, Americans are worshiping Molech, the terrible furnace god into whose fiery mouth parents in ancient times threw their children, destroying them to relieve the guilt of their own consciences. The evidence for it today is rampant in the skyrocketing cases of child abuse and child molestation, not to mention abortion murder mills.

Paul tells us how to turn from these degradations. He addresses the Thessalonians as "loved by God" (1:4). The answer to idolatry begins with an acceptance of God's love. Everything starts there. The world at large perceives God as perpetually angry, looking upon His creatures as a defiant, rebellious lot who refuse to have anything to do with Him and who ignore His teachers and suppress His Word. But God does not look at our lost race that way. The truth is found in John 3:16: "God so *loved* the world that he gave his one and only Son." He sees us as victims, deluded and deceived. Alluring philosophies have throttled our love and captivated and gripped our minds. Almost in total ignorance we pursue

the things that destroy us. Most of us have already seriously
messed up our lives. But then we learn the incredible truth
that despite our failures God loves us, and that He gave His
only begotten Son for us. It is in the cross that we see the love
of God on exhibit. Paul so states in Romans: "God commen-
deth his love toward us, in that, while we were yet sinners,
Christ died for us" (5:8 KJV).

It is also in the Scriptures that we learn "he has chosen"
us (1 Thess. 1:4). How do you know that out of the millions
who have lived on earth He chose you? The answer is, you
began to be drawn toward God, to sense a desire for Him.
The calling of God by means of the Spirit awakens a hunger
within. If you are longing to be different, if you want to be
more than you are now, if you have tried to change and
cannot, but you want to change, if you find the words of the
gospel, the songs and hymns of Christians attractive, you are
being drawn by the Spirit! Jesus said, "No one can come to
me unless the Father who sent me draws him" (John 6:44).

When the good news came to Thessalonica, people
began to feel inside themselves a desire to have this Jesus
who would make such a tremendous change in their lives.
They responded to love and thus revealed they were the elect
of God.

Paul goes on to detail the steps necessary to God's call.
First, the gospel "came . . . not simply with words" (1:5). The
Scriptures were preached, the truth was declared. The
apostle spoke to them about the promises of God in the Old
Testament. The seventeenth chapter of Acts contains a record
of Paul's preaching in the city of Berea. He believed the
Bereans to be more noble, more open than those in Thessalonica in that they "received the word with all readiness of
mind, and searched the scriptures daily, whether those
things were so" (17:11 KJV). It is through the Word of God—

through the declaration of these great promises and the simple narrative of the story of Jesus—that men and women are awakened and moved toward God.

The second factor in God's call is His power. "Our gospel came to you not simply with words, but also with power " (v. 5). The Word becomes real, compelling, gripping. The gospel has the ability to compel because it is no mere legend or myth. Christmas is much more than a beautiful story that entrances people and helps them forget the ugliness of the present. It speaks of real events. Jesus was indeed born in Bethlehem. The shepherds did come to worship Him. The angels sang their great promise of hope. A flaming star lit the heavens with glory. All of this actually happened. Jesus did live. He did move among men. He died a felon's death upon a cross. He was raised from the dead. When the Thessalonians believed, they sensed the historicity and the power of these events and were changed. They became different people.

Also, says Paul, the gospel came "with the Holy Spirit" (v. 5). Behind the power is the reality of God Himself. His Spirit can touch and fill the human spirit. He begins to minister to our minds and our hearts from within, opening them up to understand these events.

Finally, the gospel came "with deep conviction" (v. 5), moving the wills of the Thessalonians. They acted, they did something about it: They yielded their lives to God. You may have been attending church for years. You may have been hearing the gospel, but have never opened your heart to God. That is the final, necessary step. Ultimately, the will must be moved. Jesus says, "Behold, I stand at the door [of the heart], and knock: if any man hear my voice [feels desire], and open the door [invites Him to come in], I will come in to him, and will sup with him, and he with me" (Rev. 3:20 KJV). That is what happened in Thessalonica.

This, then, is "the work of faith." Until you have actually received Christ, you have not exercised faith. You can believe the story to be true, but until it moves you to accept the Lord, to invite Him into your heart, you have not exercised faith.

THE LABOR OF LOVE

The first sign of love at work is *a changed attitude*. Instead of wearisome complaining about their afflictions, the Thessalonians found "joy given by the Holy Spirit" (v. 6). Not that there wasn't good reason to complain! These young believers were ostracized at their work, hounded out of their homes, arrested, and put into prison because of their new-found faith. But, says Paul, they had learned to see these afflictions in a new way. They saw them as privileges, given to them for Jesus' sake. The result was joy! They responded to God's love by loving Him in return and welcoming the opportunities to bear suffering for His name's sake.

Jesus taught us that the greatest commandment is to love the Lord our God. But there is always something that must come before that, something many people do not seem to understand. God asks us to love Him only because *He first loved us*. When trials, pressures, and hardships come along, we are able to see for ourselves what kind of solution God can work out. The Thessalonians had stopped complaining and started rejoicing because they saw God working through their trials. If only *we* could understand that afflictions are opportunities for God to demonstrate His sustaining grace and show His work in our lives today, we could experience the same joy they knew.

The second mark of love's labor is *sharing*. The Thessalonian believers shared the good news throughout Macedonia and Achaia (v. 7). They did not do it by means of great crusades or campaigns. There were no citywide meetings in rented stadiums.

We can do that today, and thank God for it, but that is not what the Thessalonians did. They simply told their neighbors and friends what God had done for them. They explained the new joy and peace that had come into their hearts. Then, when their friends began to ask questions, they invited them over and opened the Scriptures. Through the quiet, almost invisible, network of what we would call home Bible studies, they shared the good news. Silently, without fanfare, the gospel spread throughout this whole area of the Roman Empire. The entire countryside was stirred by what was taking place in people's lives.

In Thessalonica the city fathers described Paul and his friends by saying, "These men *who have turned the world upside down*, have come here also" (Acts 17:6 RSV). In this way the good news eventually filtered into all parts of the known world.

The third proof of love's labor was displayed by the Thessalonian believers in their *daily trust* in God's care. "Your faith in God has become known everywhere. Therefore we do not need to say anything," Paul commended them (v. 8). They believed that God was their Father and would take care of them no matter what happened.

Recently I received a letter from two missionaries in Guatemala, Ron and Gretchen Bruno. Gretchen wrote of an incident that had encouraged her greatly. A poor widow in one of the congregations in Guatemala was down to her last twenty cents and without food. She began to pray about her problem. As she was praying she felt a deep conviction that

God was telling her to go to the large supermarket in town the next day and fill up several carts with groceries and take them to checkout stand number 7. This was not just a vague feeling on her part but a deep, Spirit-born conviction. She went to the supermarket the next morning, loaded enough groceries into carts to last two or three months, and took them to checkout stand 7. Just as she got there the cashier closed the stand to go for lunch. She suggested that the woman take her groceries to another stand, but the woman said, "No, I cannot. My Father told me to take these through stand 7." So she waited until the clerk came back from lunch. The clerk was surprised to see the woman still there but started to check out her groceries. Just then an announcement came over the loudspeaker: "Since this is our seventh year of business, we are pleased to announce that whoever is checking out at checkout stand 7 will receive free groceries."

Now I am not telling you to go to your local supermarket and stand in checkout lane 7, but I am telling you to do what this woman did: trust God. Believe that He cares for you, that He is a loving heavenly Father, and that He has a thousand and one ways of meeting your needs. Although He seldom does the same thing twice, the unchangeable fact is that God loves us. We belong to Him.

The Thessalonians demonstrated that belief so effectively that their faith had been reported everywhere. They had an invisible means of support, but it was evident in their confident behavior.

THE HOPE THAT ENDURES

A striking feature about the Thessalonian letters is that each chapter in both letters ends with a reference to the

coming of the Lord. We look back to His first coming, but
among these early believers the great hope lay in His coming
again. They believed what the angels had said to the disciples
on the Mount of Olives: "This same Jesus, who has been taken
from you into heaven, will come back in the same way " (Acts
1:11). It was the ever-present hope of the early church, and
that hope became the dominant theme of the Thessalonian
letters.

Their answer to the threat of personal death was a firm
belief in Jesus' resurrection. Jesus had said, "Because I live,
you also will live" (John 14:19). Now they were to "wait for
his [God's] Son from heaven" (1:10).

The Thessalonians were confident of their victory over
death, and they did not fear what Paul calls "the coming
wrath" (1 Thess. 1:10). This is not a reference to hell. In John
5:24, Jesus had said: "Whoever hears my word and believes
him who sent me *has* eternal life and *will not be condemned;* he
has crossed over from death to life." These faithful believers
had learned from Paul that they would not face *that* judgment. Here, he is referring to a coming period of wrath on
earth. The use of the present tense indicates that it is a future
event from which they could also be assured of deliverance
by their Lord.

In the Old Testament this period is called "the terrible
day of the Lord" (Joel 2:31 KJV). It is a time when God's
judgments will rain down upon the earth. Jesus Himself
described it as the "great tribulation, such as has not been
from the beginning of the world until now, no, and never will
be" (Matt. 24:21 KJV). That time is yet ahead. But throughout
these letters we learn that God has a plan to deliver His own
from that "coming wrath." Christians shall have victory even
over the approaching crisis of the world.

More important than the certainty of heaven or escape from the agony of living is the promise that He who is coming again *even now* rules in the affairs of men. Intertwined with the promise of John 14 is the assurance that He will come to live within us. "I will not leave you as orphans," He said, "I will come to you" (v. 18). The wonderful paradox that Christians possess is that though the kingdom of Christ is yet coming when Jesus will return to this earth, He is already here with us now. He is leading us, fulfilling us, ministering to us, guarding us, and, even now, ruling in earthly affairs.

What does this mean to us today? Simply this: Christians have no business being discouraged, defeated, or despairing. If we succumb to any of these moods, it is because we have forgotten the great truths proclaimed in Paul's letter. But there in troubled Thessalonica these truths were living, vital, and fragrant in the hearts of the believers. Surely, in our dark hour of history, God is calling us back to the fundamentals of the Christian life—faith, hope, and love.

WHATEVER BECAME OF INTEGRITY?

2

(2:1–12)

A NEW PHENOMENON in America is the rise of the mega-church. When I was a boy, a church with two or three thousand members was considered rare and enormous; today, however, there are dozens of them, and they are regarded as moderate-sized. It is not uncommon to hear of a church with a congregation of ten thousand or more meeting every Sunday. In one such church, 3,500 people come together on Wednesday evenings, many of them untouched pagans. It is exciting to see the Lord at work in their midst.

Recently I attended a conference where thirty Southern California pastors met together; among those attending were both young and old men, both outgoing and retiring personalities. But their common bond was their deep concern for people. These men were real pastors and shepherds.

Guest speaker Peter Drucker, an expert on business and management, offered some comments on approaches and organization, but the main emphasis of all the discussions was how to minister to people.

In the first twelve verses of 1 Thessalonians we find a great model for ministry. The apostle Paul was a master shepherd, and while there is no doubt that Paul is here defending himself from some criticisms that had arisen after his departure from Thessalonica, there emerges in this passage a marvelous picture of the work of a good shepherd.

You may be asking, "How does this apply to me? Pastors are a special breed. Does Paul have anything to say to me?" One of the young men at the pastors' meeting commented: "Jesus was so human nobody would believe He was God, but we pastors are so godlike nobody thinks we're human!" There is an element of truth in that. But may I remind you that *every believer is in the ministry.* If you are a parent, you have a little flock at home. This passage will help you minister to them effectively. You may meet with friends at breakfast or lunch; you may hold a Bible class in your home. This passage teaches how to be effective in any ministry, how to touch and change people, how to shepherd them.

PROFILE OF AN EFFECTIVE PASTOR

The first six verses reflect one of the primary qualities of a good shepherd—*Courage!*

Courage is the first essential for helping somebody else, especially when they don't want to be helped! Do you sometimes find it hard to bring up a painful subject that needs to be discussed? Some people are very sensitive and do not like to be reminded of shortcomings and weaknesses. That is when courage is required.

Paul, of course, is referring here to physical courage. He really is understating the case when he says he had "been insulted," and that he had "suffered" in Philippi (2:2). Actually, this was one of the three times he was beaten with thick rods and then thrown into prison, a Roman form of punishment. There, although he and Silas were thrust into stocks and held immobile, they began to sing praises to God.

Furthermore, Paul had suffered insult and mockery by being stripped of his clothes in public by order of the magistrates in Philippi. His Roman citizenship had been ignored. Even when he was freed by an earthquake, he was summarily ordered out of town by the authorities.

Yet he went bravely on to Thessalonica knowing that the same thing could happen there. When a riot broke out in Ephesus, he actually tried to face down a howling mob who were bent on taking his life. He had to be restrained by his friends to keep from sacrificing himself to the mob's fury. One cannot read the life of Paul and fail to see the tremendous courage he demonstrated in his ministry.

Where did he get such courage? Some say that Paul was bold by nature, that he would take on anything or anyone. But certain verses indicate that was not true. When he came into Corinth and began to preach, he did so "in weakness and fear, and with much trembling" (1 Cor. 2:3) The Corinthians intimidated him.

Some of you who want to reach out to your fellow-workers feel intimidated at times by the pagan atmosphere of your workplace. Paul felt that very strongly. He had "conflicts on the outside, fears within" (2 Cor. 7:5). No, Paul was not naturally courageous. He was like most of us. The few times in my life that I have shown courage were simply the grace of God at work.

PAUL'S PLATFORM FOR MINISTRY

In these next verses, Paul declares very clearly, both negatively and positively, what lay behind his courage.

1. *Paul did not come preaching some private revelation;* he did not preach out of "error or impure motives" (v. 3). Today we are confronted with a parade of gurus, prophets, seers, avatars, and others, peddling their peculiar forms of doctrine. The Hare Krishnas confront you in airports; the Moonies, under the leadership of Sun Myung Moon, who claims to be the Messiah, boldly proclaim their doctrine across the country and around the world. On the surface they appear to be bold and courageous. They seem to be driven by conviction—but it is wrong conviction. Paul's message was the truth of God, confirmed by the prophets and by Jesus Christ Himself.

2. *Paul did not preach an easy gospel, nor did he preach out of impure motives* (v. 3). Some, like Jim Jones, attract great crowds of followers by encouraging them to indulge themselves, to throw over all moral restraints and do whatever they wish. The Bhagwan commune in Oregon participated in sexual orgies and people flocked there, attracted by that kind of degenerate teaching. But this was never part of the apostle's doctrine.

3. *Paul did not use guile nor flattery to win converts* (v. 5). I appreciate his words along that line, when so many teachers today are appealing to our egos, to the macho instinct in us. They seem to be bold and uncompromising in their approach, but they manifest every indication of sheer ego and

disguise it by appearing to be simple teachers of the Word. What they are teaching has a degree of truth to it, but it is mixed with a great deal of error. Tragically, many succumb to that kind of appeal.

4. *Paul did not promise prosperity in exchange for discipleship.* Some entice followers with the offer of a formula for success and wealth. This was not Paul's method. "Nor did we put on a mask to cover up greed" (v. 5). What an apt description of much we hear today!

Paul would have nothing to do with this type of appeal. As we will see, he refused even to accept financial support from the Thessalonians, earning his own way as a tentmaker. He concentrated on giving them what they desperately needed—the message of the gospel—and he supported himself until they had received it.

5. *Finally, Paul did not come to seek praise or status in the eyes of man* (v. 6). He could have played upon his position as an authorized spokesman of Jesus, but he did not want anything for himself. He did not slant his message, slurring over some of the unpleasant aspects of the truth, to appeal to the popular mind. He was honest and faithful, and ministered to them truthfully, regardless of whether he received any praise, glory, or thanks. None of these motives lay behind his preaching—not error, uncleanness, guile, flattery, greed, or ambition.

TO PLEASE GOD ALONE

What did motivate Paul, then? What produced his kind of courage? We learn the answer in verse 4: "We speak as men approved by God to be entrusted with the gospel. We are not trying to please men but God, who tests our hearts."

First, he is intensely grateful for the sheer honor of proclaim
ing the gospel, the good news about God. Four times in these
verses (in vv. 2, 4, 8, and 9) he mentions the gospel of God.
He gloried in the fact that God had called him to deliver a
message that people needed so desperately.

Why do people suffer heartbreak, loneliness, misery,
and agony of spirit day in and day out throughout their lives?
It is because they do not know the truth about God. They do
not know the delivering power of Jesus Christ. They do not
know the inner warmth, strength, and encouragement that
can come from Christ living in them. God committed that
message to Paul, and He also commits it to us so that we
might share it with others. What an honor that is! In all my
years of preaching nothing has been more encouraging to me
than to remind myself that I have already been given the
greatest honor that can ever be given to a human being: to
proclaim what Paul calls "the unsearchable riches of Christ."
Could there be anything greater than that? That is how Paul
felt, and it continually motivated him.

More than that, Paul was energized by a desire to please
God. Now the only reason anyone has a desire to please God
is because he has learned to love Him. You never truly try to
please God if you do not love God. You may try to please
Him to get something for yourself, but if the impelling force
within you is to please Him, it is because you have learned
that God already loves you. That is why we sing so many
hymns that speak about the love of God for us. Every Christian ought to recall regularly that fantastic deed when

> *On Christ almighty vengeance fell,*
> *That would have sunk a world to hell.*
> *He bore it for a chosen race,*
> *And thus became our hiding place.*

That is what drives us to want to please God.

Certainly love was always Jesus' motive for performance. He said so Himself: "I do always those things which please my Father." He did not live and act as He did because He wanted something from God—all the treasures of heaven could have been His at any moment—but because He loved the Father and wanted to please Him.

Bold, blustery Peter had a powerful experience with the Lord after the resurrection when he met Him by the Sea of Galilee. Three times Jesus asked him the searching question: "Peter, do you love me?" Finally, all Peter could say was, "Lord, you know that I love you" (John 21:15-17). Love brought Peter back from the moment of his disobedience and weakness. He knew that he loved Jesus, because Jesus had first loved him.

Love is truly the wellspring of courage. Do not try to summon courage from within yourself. Think about the love of God, the honor of walking with Him, and speaking the truth to others. Soon you will find yourself driven—or compelled, as Paul puts it in 2 Corinthians 5:14—by "Christ's love." That is the secret of his courageous activity.

THE GOOD SHEPHERD

In addition to courage, there are other qualities necessary in one who shepherds people. Paul's words reflect his own shepherd heart.

Gentle Nurturer

The apostle uses a beautiful metaphor in his next words when he describes himself as a mother "caring for her little children" (1 Thess. 2:7). There is a time for tough love, of course, but even then the sensitive shepherd finds ways to administer it gently. This love deeply desires to bless others and expresses concern tenderly.

When I was a young Christian, I came under the ministry of Dawson Trotman, the founder of the Navigators. A strong personality, Dawson could be demanding. He was self-disciplined to an enormous degree, and he expected self-discipline of those who worked with him. But when I met alone with Dawson, he was always gentle. He spoke directly to me and seemed aware of my need and my capacity. I often thought of him as being like the apostle Paul. Paul could be stern and sharp, but when he was with someone alone, he was gentle. Gentleness is a mark of a true shepherd.

"Being affectionately desirous of you" (v. 8 RSV) is an unusual phrase, not often found in Scripture. Literally it means "a yearning, a longing for you." I sometimes feel this myself, especially when I am talking with a young person. I feel my heart longing to help them, to bless them, to teach them, to lead them, to fulfill them. That is how parents feel about their children. There is a yearning after them, an affectionate desire to see them blossom and grow in the right direction.

Diligent Laborer

A shepherd's life is not an easy life. "You remember, brothers, our toil and hardship; we worked night and day in order not to be a burden to anyone" (v. 9).

Paul knew the meaning of hard work. Every Jewish boy had to learn a trade, and Paul's trade was tentmaking. Rather than take offerings from his new converts, he worked long hours into the night to earn his own living. Perhaps as they listened to him teaching and instructing them during the daytime, the Thessalonians noticed that Paul's hands were not the cultured, soft hands of a rich man who had never done manual labor. They were, rather, the calloused hands of one who worked hard at his trade.

My wife thinks her hands are ugly because they are not as smooth and soft as they once were. But to me her hands are beautiful because they represent self-sacrificing labor. Long hours doing dishes and mopping floors may take their toll, but work-worn hands reflect a loving heart.

Faithful Servant

Faithfulness is probably the most important mark of a good shepherd. The modern term *integrity* accurately expresses this. Paul was not boasting, only reporting fact when he claimed to be "holy, righteous, and blameless" (v. 10).

Holiness means "separate, intended for a single purpose." In this sense, "single-minded" would be a good translation. The Old Testament speaks of the beauty of holiness, of someone who knows to whom he belongs and is satisfied. Many think Paul was an egotist, a boaster who claimed things he had no right to claim. But whenever he spoke of his own holiness, Paul made clear that he was not responsible for it. It was the grace of God at work in him.

Also Paul was *righteous* before others. He behaved himself, resisting activities that could be misconstrued or would tend to mislead. In Corinthians he wrote that if his drinking wine or eating meat offended, he would touch neither again. He was upright in his public behavior.

Finally, Paul was *blameless* in his own eyes. Do not misunderstand. Paul was not claiming sinlessness. What he meant was that he was honest. He had dealt with all his sin. Aware of it, he had not engaged in a cover-up, but had confessed it and received the forgiveness of God.

Recently a group of Southern California pastors met in small groups to discuss and share with one another how we keep ourselves vital and spiritually alive. One of the pastors I met with particularly intrigued me. Only thirty-five years old, this man ministers to more than ten thousand people every Sunday morning. I was interested in what he had to say about maintaining his spiritual vitality. Every morning he sits at his desk and writes across the top of a sheet of paper the letters A-C-T-S. The A stands for adoration; C, confession; T, thanksgiving; and S, supplication.

Under the letter A, he writes down all he can think of about the majesty, greatness, and glory of God. He does what Jesus teaches us to do in the Lord's Prayer—to turn our thoughts to God first: "Our Father in heaven, hallowed be your name" (Matt. 6:9). Then he contemplates the majesty of God, the greatness of His being, the love of His heart, the mercy He has manifested toward him, and the young man lists all those qualities. That is what the Psalmist did: "Praise the LORD, O my soul, and forget not all his benefits." (Ps. 103:2).

Next he turns to confession, under C. "I write down the sins that I am aware of committing yesterday," he said. "If it is Monday morning, and in my preaching Sunday I exaggerated in an illustration—I said it was a nine-car pile-up when it was only a six-car pile-up—I do not write that I exaggerated, but that I lied to the people. If I inadvertently kept some change that was given to me by mistake, I do not write down that I kept some money yesterday. I want to be hard on myself. I want to put it down in the worst possible way so I will face in myself these tendencies. I write, 'I stole some money.'

"Next," he said, "I turn to thanksgiving, under T, and I begin to give thanks that I am forgiven for these sins. One by one I cross them out and write, 'forgiven, forgiven.' Then under supplication, S, I pray and ask God for the strength not to do it again, but to be honest, careful, and thoughtful."

No wonder that young man is being greatly used of God. My heart was delighted that such a young preacher would have such integrity. That is what we see here in Paul—thorough, ruthless honesty.

From that base of a faithful personal life, the apostle does three things for the Thessalonians. He *exhorts* them, he *encourages* them, and he *challenges them*.

Exhortation usually takes the form of a rebuke. As I look back on the days when my children were growing up, I recall times when I had to sit down with them and say, "You are headed for trouble. If you go down the path you are traveling now, you are going to hurt yourself and your family. You are going to destroy things of value in your life." A father has to do that. So does a pastor at times. And so will you if you want to minister to someone's needs.

But along with exhortation come encouragement and challenge. I have to confess, as I look back on my relationships with my children, there was not enough of that. Encouragement says, "You are doing better. I can see changes. You are going to make it. I am with you. Keep on." Encouragement is pointing out the positive: "You are meant for better things. You do not have to live like this. There are great possibilities before you. God is leading you and calling you and urging you to lay hold of those." That is what Paul does here, pointing out that it is God who calls us into His own kingdom and glory.

These are surely the "times that try men's souls." But these are also times of great possibilities. What a challenge to live today as Paul lived and ministered in his day! As I review his record and see his courage, his loving, gentle spirit, and his faithfulness, I have to pray, "Lord, make me a blessing in my own time."

THE MYSTERIOUS WORD

3

(2:13–16)

*I*N THE MIDST OF flux and change, one thing remains absolutely unchangeable—the Word of the living God. The message of the Bible never alters. It is always up-to-date, speaking to the issues of every age. The Bible is like a solid rock in the midst of a desert of shifting sand. It is the most precious object on the earth today. Abraham Lincoln called it "God's best gift to man." Daniel Webster said, "If we abide by the principles taught in the Bible, our country will go on prospering . . . . But if we or our posterity neglect it and its instructions and authority, no man can tell how sudden a catastrophe may overwhelm us and bury all our glory in profound obscurity." Those are prophetic words for these times.

Paul's first letter to the Thessalonians contains a profound statement of truth about God's Word: "That you accepted it not as the word of men, but as it actually is, the word of God, which is at work in you who believe" (2:13).

In parallel with other passages, this verse declares that the Word of God is indeed a most remarkable instrument. No other verse in the Bible states so clearly and obviously that the Word of God comes to us through ordinary human beings. God's Word became flesh, became a man, to communicate with us in terms we can understand. Throughout history, God has always communicated through human beings who look, talk, and behave just like we do.

The Gospels report only three occasions on which God spoke directly to people, astounding those who heard and paralyzing them with fear. When Jesus was baptized, God spoke aloud. When our Lord was on the Mount of Transfiguration with Peter, James, and John, God spoke to them directly. Again, during that fatal last week in Jerusalem when Jesus announced that He was about to die, the Father spoke from the heavens.

But more often He has used human instruments.

Jeremiah said that the Word of God came to him like a "burning in his bones." He was compelled to utter the message; he could not keep quiet about it.

Elijah declared that the Word of God came to him like "a still small voice," though it probably was not a voice at all but a quiet realization that God was speaking within.

Daniel said that God spoke to him in "visions and dreams in the night," and he went on to interpret those strange and marvelous visions.

Moses said that when God addressed him, it was "face-to-face, like a man speaks with his friends"—a communication so clear that it seemed as if God were speaking directly to him. As a result, Moses wrote the first five books of our Bible.

The apostle Peter proclaimed that "men spoke from God as they were carried along by the Holy Spirit" (2 Peter 1:21).

It was this kind of experience that confronted the Thessalonian Christians. Paul stood up and began to speak, and as he spoke his listeners were conscious that what they were hearing was far more than the words of a mere man. They were hearing the Word of God, and they received it as such.

The greatest of all revelations, of course, was that moment when Jesus was born in Bethlehem. A great star hung over the sleeping village, dropping its silver glory upon the waiting earth. The shepherds heard the voice of angels. Troubled and puzzled, they came to a dark cave in the hillside and found a mother and her child. John writes that it was then "the word became flesh and made his dwelling among us. We have seen his glory" (1:14). The book of Hebrews declares this event to be the final and ultimate revelation of God to man: "In the past God spoke to our forefathers through the prophets at many times and in various ways, but in these last days he has spoken to us by his Son" (1:1–2). Nothing can supersede that ultimate revelation.

This raises a problem, of course, because if the Word of God comes through ordinary people, it can easily be imitated. False prophets can claim that their phony, fraudulent expressions are also the Word of God.

History catalogues a long parade of false prophets, charlatans, and kooks, all of whom have claimed to speak a message from God. The Mormon prophet, Joseph Smith, insisted that an angel named Moroni appeared to him. Later, he said he was given special spectacles to enable him to read a language written on golden tablets that he would find buried in a hillside. Many people believe him, even though the book he wrote is vastly different from the Bible in its teachings.

In our own day, thousands of people claim that God speaks directly to them and gives them a so-called "word of knowledge" about what is going on in someone else's life. This phenomenon has even been displayed on television.

GOD'S WORD IS ABSOLUTELY ACCURATE

How can we tell when God has really spoken and when we are hearing from a false prophet? The Scripture does not leave us without help in discerning the true from the false.

First, we must remember that God's actions in the world always agree with His words. The Bible states that God is its author, and that He is also the Maker of the physical universe and all the forces that are at work. He is the Controller, the King, the Lord over all of history and the affairs of men. If this is true, then we can expect experience to confirm what the Word says. History testifies to the fact that God never acts contrary to His Word. Thus, if someone promises something that the Word of God does not promise, we can know immediately that we have heard false teaching.

Furthermore, when a prophet, man or woman, predicts that a certain future event will occur and it does not happen, the Bible declares that person to be a false prophet; the prophecy is to be disregarded, since it is not the Word of God. Yet the Bible makes the amazing claim that every one of its predictions is 100 percent accurate. Measured by that standard, some of the secular forecasts we hear today are rather ridiculous.

Every year the *National Enquirer* publishes the predictions of contemporary psychics for the coming year. I buy and keep that edition of the paper just to see how many of them are borne out. You may be interested to know that included among those made in January for the year 1987 were the following: One psychic predicted that the Russian leader Gorbachev would be assassinated on May 1 during a celebration of the Russian Revolution. Another claimed that Khadaffi, the Libyan dictator, would be shot by one of his own guards and left paralyzed. Still another forecast that Michael Jackson would leave his musical career to become a TV evangelist. Those false predictions mark the prophets who made them as phonies who are not to be trusted. Many people have followed Jeanne Dixon, but her batting average is only about 40 percent; the same measure of accuracy could be attained with good guesses.

One of the clear marks of the Word of God is that it is absolutely accurate. It accords with reality. Recently a young man said to me, "I recommitted my life to Christ this year, because I have come to see that the Bible is true. This is the way God runs His world. Anything less is not to be trusted."

GOD'S WORD PRODUCES CHANGE

The apostle Paul suggests another way to test reality, found in the phrase at the end of verse 13: "the word of God, *which is at work* in you who believe." Merely to memorize Bible verses or even to mentally accept the truth found in them does not change anyone. It is only as people begin to act on the Word and to obey it that they are radically and permanently changed. The Word will then make them into different people. The Bible itself makes that claim: "For the word of God is living and active. Sharper than any double-edged sword, it penetrates even to dividing soul and spirit, joints and marrow; it judges the thoughts and attitudes of the heart" (Heb. 4:12).

God, through His Word, analyzes our motives, enables us to confess to wrong thinking, then corrects that thinking. "All Scripture is inspired by God [breathed out by God] and is profitable [useful] for teaching [instructing you about things you could never know otherwise], for reproof [telling you what has gone wrong in your life], for correction [helping you make necessary changes], and for training in righteousness [the practical guidelines to truth: how to react to situations, how to handle your anger, your sex drive, etc.]" (2 Tim. 3:16 RSV).

Most of us are familiar with the story of the mutiny on the *Bounty*. In the nineteenth century, crew members of the HMS *Bounty* took over the ship, set their captain adrift in a lifeboat, and ended up at last on Pitcairn Island in the South Pacific. But that is only part of the story. What happened to the mutineers after they landed is something else altogether. These rough, tough, godless sailors, together with the wives they had taken with them from the island of Tahiti, spent their days on Pitcairn drinking, gambling, carousing, and fighting among themselves. Soon the fighting led to battle. One by one they killed each other off until the colony was reduced to a handful of people. Among them was a man named Alexander Smith. Rummaging through his trunk one day, Smith found a Bible that his mother had put there. He began to read it, and his life was changed. As he read to the survivors a dramatic change began taking place in their lives as well, and when that island was discovered by outsiders some years later, the inhabitants had become a model community. There was no jail because there was no crime. The citizens loved God and each other. The Book had totally changed their lives and their society.

GOD'S WORD AROUSES OPPOSITION

The apostle says that this wonderful life-changing Word has another remarkable power—the power to arouse violent opposition: "You suffered from your own countrymen the same things those churches suffered from the Jews, who killed the Lord Jesus and the prophets and also drove us out. They displease God and are hostile to all men in their effort to keep us from speaking to the Gentiles so that they may be saved" (2:14–15).

Throughout history, every generation of Christians has known persecution and martyrdom. Christians have been bound in animal skins and left to die in the hot sun, thrown into lions' dens, burned alive, and exiled. Why such violent opposition to this remarkable Word with its power to bless and transform? There are three major reasons.

First, it is clear from the Scriptures that *the gospel ignores all human achievement.* God is totally unimpressed with degrees, awards, position, tenure, wealth, or any other trappings of power. Even religious achievements, a good set of moral values, and a strong belief system are not sufficient to earn spiritual merit. All must come to God in the same simple way: by admitting they cannot help themselves and by accepting salvation as a gift from the hand of God through Jesus Christ. Jesus Himself declared, "No one comes to the Father except through me" (John 14:6). You may believe in God, but you will never know Him as Father unless you come through Jesus. As the old hymn puts it, "Nothing in my hand I bring, simply to Thy cross I cling."

Other religions find this claim to be offensive. Why I do not know, because much of life is lived out on that practical level. We cannot make up our own rules about many things. The laws of electricity must be carefully observed before we dare to tinker with electrical current. Telephone numbers must be dialed in the correct sequence before a connection is made with the party we are calling. We do not have the freedom to arrange the numbers to our own liking; we must get them just right.

God insists that there is only one way to be reconciled with Him, and that is through Jesus Christ. That makes a lot of people very angry. But whether Buddhists or Muslims, Baptists, Methodists or Presbyterians, religious performance does nothing to impress God. Neither will it change us. The only thing that can change us is the Word of God, received by faith.

The second reason the gospel arouses violent opposition is that *it exposes human pride*. There is a terrible evil in all of us that we try to hide. I find it in myself. For example, I am stubborn at times, and I excuse myself on the grounds that people need to be stubborn occasionally. Besides, I am half Scot and the Scots are known for stubbornness. But that is nothing but pride—an independent spirit that says, "I don't need any help. I can make it on my own." We are all guilty of this in varying degrees, but we keep it under control for fear of recrimination or out of a desire not to be known as prideful or stubborn. If the restraints are removed, however, that pride will suddenly break out in the most terrible form of viciousness and vindictiveness.

What a vivid demonstration we had of this in the destruction of PSA Flight 1771 in California, between Los Angeles and San Jose. In this instance, an individual whose heart was seething with hatred for another man, whom he imagined had wronged him, took a gun and murdered the man. In the process he also killed the pilots of the plane, causing the plane to crash, and forty-two other passengers perished in the crash.

That is how terrible human pride can be. But the gospel exposes that sin in us and shows us how hideous it is in the eyes of God. The book of Proverbs tells us that there are seven things God hates, and number one on the list is "a proud look"—a self-sufficient spirit, an independent trust in one's own powers.

Perhaps an old hymn best expresses how we must approach God:

> *I heard the voice of Jesus say,*
> *"Behold, I freely give*
> *The living water; thirsty one,*
> *Stoop down and drink, and live."*
> *I came to Jesus and I drank*
> *Of that life-giving stream;*
> *My thirst was quenched, my heart revived,*
> *And now I live in Him.*

The key is the phrase "stoop down." You cannot receive living water unless you are willing to stoop down, to humble yourself and admit you do not have it yourself. There is no other hope, no other way. You must admit you cannot save yourself.

A third reason the gospel arouses opposition is because *it forgives blatant sinners*—those who richly deserve death and hell in the eyes of the world. The Pharisees were very offended because Jesus received adulterers, prostitutes, swindlers, and outcasts, while they themselves, respectable moral people, were excluded. That is why they finally killed Jesus.

Many oppose the gospel because it makes appeal to the disreputable. But that is its glory: it can change anyone who will receive it in humility and contrition.

THE CUP OF WRATH

God sometimes takes severe measures to awaken people to their situation before "[his] wrath comes upon them at last!" (v. 16 RSV).

Paul knew what was coming. He makes reference to the dark cloud of national disaster that was hanging over Israel at this time. As he wrote this letter the Roman armies were already being hassled by Jewish rebellion. Before long the soldiers would lay siege to Jerusalem and finally break down its walls, destroy the temple, take the Jews captive, and lead them out into dispersion among the nations of the earth. God had patiently waited while His stubborn people heaped "up to the limit their sins" (2:16).

God is not an angry, vindictive Being who hurls thunderbolts of judgment at the slightest provocation. No, He gives us a chance to wake up and see what is happening to us; He patiently, mercifully waits for us to change. But if we do not, there comes a time when He forces us to live with the consequences as a last-ditch measure to open our eyes to reality.

That is happening in our world today. In response to the AIDS crisis, we are hearing much about so-called "safe sex." People are being told that it is possible, by using certain safeguards, to have what is called "safe sex" and avoid pregnancy or disease. But according to the Scripture, there can be no such thing as "safe sex" outside of marriage. Though pregnancy and disease may be prevented by taking certain measures, what cannot be evaded is the moral disaster brought on by sexual promiscuity. "For because of such things," the apostle says, "God's wrath comes on those who are disobedient" (Eph. 5:6). It cannot be avoided; there is no way of escape. There is no way to "have it all" and yet avoid that final reckoning of God's judgment. There is no way, ultimately, to escape the effects of individual promiscuous living upon society. Instead of finding liberty and freedom, as is promised, what we have instead is child abuse, rape, violence, serial murders, drug abuse, and rocketing teenage suicide.

These are sobering words, reminding us that we live in perilous times. Those of us who know the Lord Jesus must not allow ourselves to become caught up in the shallow expressions of the world. Let us continually give grateful thanks for the gift of Jesus Christ our Lord. And let us continually spread the good news: To you who cannot save yourselves, to you who are already perishing because of the forces at work in your life over which you have no control, "to you is born this day . . . a Savior, who is Christ the Lord" (Luke 2:11 RSV).

A
FATHER'S 4
JOY
(2:17–3:13)

*R*EAL FATHER LOVE is in short supply in our world today. What we see is a frightening increase of child abuse, of fathers actually attacking their own children. Some time ago I read the sad story of a four-year-old boy who was beaten to death by his stepfather because the boy had wet his pants. When the small body was dug up, a tiny cross was found clutched in his hand.

No aspect of Christian faith warms my heart more than knowing that God is my Father. Since I lost my own father when I was only ten years old, it has been a tremendous encouragement to know that the church is, after all, a family, and that God is our great Father and tenderly cares for us. On one occasion when Jesus was informed that His mother and brothers were waiting for Him, He said of the disciples He was teaching, "These are my mother and father and brother," thereby indicating that a spiritual tie is as rich and as deep as a physical tie.

A FATHER'S CONCERN

First Thessalonians 2:17 is a great testimony to a father's love. Here the apostle, as their spiritual father, pours out his concern for the new Christians he has left in Thessalonica. "But brothers, when we were torn away from you . . . out of our intense longing we made every effort to see you. For we wanted to come to you . . . again and again" (2:17).

How can anyone reading these words believe that Paul was stern and cold? His letter overflows with the warmth of his heart and the depth of his love for his children in the faith. At the time, Paul was ministering alone in the city of Corinth, no doubt feeling lonely and distant from those he loved so dearly. Forgetting the danger that had driven him from Thessalonica and the cruelty he had experienced there, he longed to be with those friends again. Still, when he tried to see them, "Satan stopped" him.

Satanic Hindrance

Have you ever experienced a frustrating time in your own life when again and again you tried to do something you knew was right and found it hard going? Perhaps the opposition came from your own family or even from members of the family of God, the church. That is satanic hindrance: the psychological manipulation Satan uses to plant obstacles in your path.

On a visit to Northern Ireland, my wife and I spent some time in a wonderful church where a young pastor and his wife were beginning to teach Body Life and Spiritual War-fare. Once theirs had been a lifeless church; now it was thriving, filled with young people and young couples. But while we were visiting, we learned that the best friend of the pastor and his wife had suddenly turned against them and had begun to spread lies about them throughout the con-gregation, upsetting the whole church. It was a terrible time of pain and suffering for them. We have since learned that God has cleared it all up and the pastor has been vindicated. But what caused such a state of confusion in the first place? It was satanic opposition, the Devil using his clever ability to work through people to stir things up.

The Bible is the only book that explains the persistence and malevolence of evil. Why do we struggle so in this life? What are we up against? Jesus tells us that it is the Devil. "He is a liar and a murderer." He deceives and he kills. The satanic mind is responsible for all the murderous violence, the widespread deceit, and the false philosophies that confront us today. Paul himself tells us, "Our struggle is not against flesh and blood but against the rulers, against the authorities, against the powers of this dark world and against the spiritual forces of evil in the heavenly realms" (Eph. 6:12). No other book reveals this truth: that it is not people who are the problem, but the spiritual forces of evil that prevail in the world.

Paul suggests in his writings that there are three things we need to know about this reality. First, and perhaps most important, *satanic opposition is permitted by God*. In the book of Job we learn that Satan had to ask God for permission to afflict Job's body. Job lost everything—his family, his home, and even his health. But God allowed it to happen. The end of the book reveals what was accomplished by that suffering, but for the moment it was all hidden from Job's eyes. So, too, the purpose of suffering and opposition is often hidden from our eyes. But the Bible reveals that there is a malevolent power of evil at work. There are demonic beings, master manipulators, that are permitted to lead people about, putting thoughts in their minds and planting obstacles in the path of the gospel.

Satanic opposition is permitted for this reason—to be used by God. Opposition is an effective method of training. Affliction, suffering, pain, and heartache are often God's way of getting our attention. You may have paid little attention to Him until you suffered a time of great distress; then you began to hear what He was saying to you. God uses opposition not only to train us, but to give us an opportunity to overcome trouble, to rise above it.

Satanic opposition underscores the value of believers. "For what is our hope, our joy, or the crown in which we will glory in the presence of our Lord Jesus when he comes? Is it not you? Indeed, you are our glory and joy" (1 Thess. 2:19). Whatever else those words may mean, they are saying that Paul considered the spiritual maturing of these believers in Thessalonica and other places his most important work. He was saying, "I have invested my life in you and your growth into mature, whole people. This is the most important thing in the world. When the Lord Jesus comes, I will glow with pride that you have achieved the changes in your life that I so longed to see brought about."

Toward Christian Maturity

Every morning my wife and I read a fine devotional book which has been collected from the writings of Dr. J. I. Packer. Recently we read a section where he quoted what a psychologist had said about the six marks of maturity—what it means to be grown up, to be whole, balanced, sane, and able to cope with life.

The first mark of maturity is the ability to deal constructively with reality, to face facts, to resist covering, or calling reality something else, to deal with it as it is. Mature people do not kid themselves.

The second mark is the ability to adapt quickly to change. We all experience change, whether it be physical, emotional, spiritual, mental, relational, or vocational. Immature people resist change; it makes them nervous. But the mark of maturity is to adapt to change because change is inevitable.

The third mark is freedom from the symptoms of tension and anxiety. The worried look, the frown, the ulcers, the palpitations of the heart—all come from anxiety and worry and lack of trust. Maturing means you have begun to see that God is in control of this world. He is working out purposes that you do not always understand, but accept. He will take you through the deep water, not drown you in it. Maturity means you are learning to trust.

Fourth, maturity is being more satisfied with giving than receiving. When you find greater joy in the thoughtful planning of gifts and surprises for others, anticipating their happiness rather than your own, it is a sign you are growing up. You are discovering the true values of life.

The fifth mark is the ability to relate to others with consistency, helpfulness, and mutual satisfaction. Maturity is learning to get along with other people, to be a help not a hindrance, to contribute to the solution and not always be a part of the problem.

Finally, maturity is the ability to sublimate and redirect anger toward constructive ends. Maturity is the ability to use the adrenaline created by anger in a positive way, rather than to lose your temper and add to the problem. That is what the apostle longed for in these believers in Thessalonica.

A FATHER'S COMMITMENT

As this passage makes clear, Paul's concern for the Thessalonian Christians also took the form of a deep commitment to them.

Twice the apostle refers to a time while he was in Athens when he "could stand it no longer" (3:1). That does not mean that he was anxious and fearful. Rather, he had not heard from his friends for so long that he felt he must take some action to find out what was going on in Thessalonica. To his own personal deprivation he decided to send Timothy to them while he remained alone in Athens and then went on to Corinth.

In 1960 I spent the summer in the Orient. In company with Dr. Dick Hillis I was scheduled to speak to six hundred Chinese pastors on the island of Taiwan. This was a difficult assignment since my messages were to be interpreted into two different languages, Mandarin and Taiwanese. It is hard enough speaking through one "interrupter," but with two, by the time one sentence has been interpreted twice you have forgotten what you just said. But I was comforted by the fact that Dick Hillis, a veteran missionary, would be with me. The day before I was due to speak, however, Dick received a telegram saying that his mother was ill and he had to return home to California. I have never forgotten the depression and loneliness that came over me.

I am sure that is how Paul must have felt as he was left alone in Corinth, that cultured, decadent center of Roman life. He had to face the city by himself, but he was willing to do it so that these Thessalonian believers could grow in their faith.

In sending Timothy to them, Paul had three things in mind, he tells us. First, *"to establish you in your faith"* (v. 2 RSV); that is, to teach them the great realities their faith rested upon—the coming of Jesus, His life and ministry, His death upon the cross, His resurrection, the coming of the Holy Spirit, and thus the availability of a new resource in God that the world could not know anything about. The Thessalonians needed to be established in that truth, and that was Timothy's mission.

Second, Paul hoped that Timothy would *"exhort"* *them to steadiness,* so "that no one be moved by these afflictions" (v. 3 RSV). They needed to know that panic was not the appropriate response to problems, and that suffering and affliction could be overcome. These believers had a new source of strength, so there was no need to fear. They could now lean on God. He would take them through everything and use it for their benefit.

Paul had already laid the foundation for this truth when he was with the Thessalonians. He had warned them "beforehand" (v. 4 RSV) that the human race was contaminated with a terrible pollution that the Bible calls sin.

The great plague of our day is AIDS, an acronym for Acquired Immune Deficiency Syndrome. I think that sin, too, is an acronym. It stands for Self-Inflicted Neurosis. Sin is a problem that arises from within. Jesus said, "Out of the heart proceed evil thoughts, murders, adulteries, fornications, thefts, false witness, blasphemies" (Matt. 15:19 KJV). Sin is an internal contaminant that we inherit at birth. The bad news is that "the wages of sin is death"—pain, suffering, anguish, alienation. But with it always comes the good news: "The gift of God is eternal life in Jesus Christ our Lord" (Rom. 6:23).

We cannot evade the painful results of our sinful choices, but we can find love, joy, and peace even while working through them.

This is the good news! This is what Paul had taught the Thessalonians, and Timothy was sent to remind them of this and to encourage them to remain steadfast in the face of adversity and affliction.

The third reason Paul sent Timothy was that *he himself needed to know what was going on.* When Timothy returned with such a good report, the apostle was filled with joy. "We were encouraged about you because of your faith . . . . For now we really live, since you are standing firm in the Lord. How can we thank God enough for you in return for all the joy we have in the presence of our God because of you?" (vv. 7–9).

To Paul's great relief, his work had not been in vain. It stood solid and sure. The faith of his followers was intact; their love was evident; and best of all, their trust in God was secure. They held cherished memories of the apostle and longed to see him. He was filled with thankfulness and joy at this good news—always the effect upon a father's heart when he receives good reports of his children in the faith. John, too, wrote of this in his third letter: "I have no greater joy than to hear that my children are walking in the truth" (v. 4).

I can testify to that fact. My wife and I have been observing a dear young man who is going through the possible disintegration of his marriage. It is a painful time for him. His home is broken, his children have been taken away, but that very suffering has brought him to an awareness of his own contribution to the problem. He is seeing himself in a new light and is becoming aware of his mistakes. Though our hearts ache for him, we are also rejoicing because we see that he is discovering a new plateau of faith. In the midst of his agony he is experiencing joy. He has even expressed gratitude that this tragedy has happened, since it has brought him to his senses and into a new relationship with God. Paul must have felt much the same when Timothy reported on the trials and testings of the Thessalonians.

HOW TO PRAY FOR YOUR CHILDREN

Do you ever wonder how to pray when you, your family, or your friends are going through deep struggles and sorrow? Romans 8:26 reminds us that at times we do not know how we ought to pray, but the Spirit helps us! God has promised such help. Here we have a good example of how the Spirit helped the apostle to pray for exactly what the Thessalonian Christians needed.

Paul prayed "earnestly" (v. 10). He did not get down beside the bed at night and glibly say, "Bless my friends in Thessalonica." Many people pray like the man who said, "Bless me and my wife, our son John and his wife; us four and no more." But Paul considered seriously what these people were going through. He set the problem before God, and reminded Him of His promises. He took time to meditate on their needs.

Paul prayed frequently—"night and day" (v. 10). Morning and evening, while he was working on his tents, while he was walking the streets of the city, his prayers flowed out of a heart of concern and love. The believers in Thessalonica were seldom out of his thoughts, and whenever he thought of them, he prayed.

Finally, Paul prayed specifically (vv. 10–13). He had some definite prayer requests—five of them, in fact.

1. He longed to see them "face to face" (RSV). He desired to get back to Thessalonica once more to have the joy of seeing his dear friends.

2. He wanted to minister further to them "that we may . . . supply what is lacking in your faith." The Thessalonians needed to know a great deal more about the Christian view of the world and of life. When we understand how to look at the events of life from the perspective of the Word of God, we are being realistic. All the confusion and illusion disappear and we can begin to see things the way they really are.

3. He prayed to overcome satanic hindrance: "Our God and Father himself and our Lord Jesus clear the way for us to come to you." Are you finding it difficult to get where you want to go? Paul shows us how to pray: that God will open a way, either physically or spiritually, to the intended goal. Jesus said, "Ask and it will be given to you; seek and you will find; knock and the door will be opened to you" (Matt. 7:7). That is how Paul prayed. He knocked on this closed door, asking that he might get back to Thessalonica. Later accounts reveal that God answered that prayer and he did return to these believers.

4. He prayed that their love might increase. According to the New Testament, this is the mark of a successful church.

I meet frequently with pastors from all over the country, and they often talk about success in the ministry. But their measure of success is often the number of church members or the size and design of the church building. There are some famous church buildings in this country that are advertised all over the land, and people travel far just to see them. But in the New Testament, success is gauged by how much people learn to love each other, forgive one another, listen to one another, support and pray for one another, and reach out to those in need around them. That is what Paul prayed for the Thessalonians.

5. He prayed that they might continue to live righteously until the Lord comes: "May he strengthen your hearts so that you will be blameless and holy in the presence of our God and Father when our Lord Jesus comes with all his holy ones" (v. 13). The coming of Jesus is no further away for you and me than it was for the believers in Thessalonica, since it is no further away than the end of your life or mine. He comes for us, if we know Him when we die. Paul therefore prayed that the rest of their lives might be marked by "unblamable" living.

Unblamable does not mean sinless, as we have already seen; *unblamable* means dealing with what is wrong, not covering it up or pretending it is not there. The Thessalonian Christians dealt with sin in their hearts with the spiritual resources provided by God, and thus were enabled to turn from evil and walk closer and closer with the Father.

Paul knew that Jesus Christ would someday enter into this world of time again. The Scripture anticipates it. We are perhaps nearing the time of His return right now. It could occur before the end of this century. Though His second coming is no further away than our own personal death, it may be even sooner than that. Paul prayed that all believers would live in the expectation that the Lord's coming would find them living the way they ought to live.

I have observed that most Christians pray that God will prevent certain things from happening, whether it be injury, death, suffering, or heartache. Unfortunately, there are people who teach that we have a right to be spared all trouble. But the New Testament shows us that afflictions are needed in our lives. God does sometimes grant our requests and remove problems—and it is not wrong to pray in this way if we also understand that He has perfect freedom to say no; but He prefers that we pray, not for negative things to be prevented, but that they be used to grow us up into Christ.

In the week before Jesus was crucified, He said to Peter, His most troublesome and outspoken apostle (the one who suffered most from hoof-in-mouth disease), "Simon, Satan has asked to sift you as wheat. But I have prayed for you . . . " (Luke 22:31–32). He did not pray, "Do not let it happen. Stop Satan from getting hold of Peter." Rather, what He said was, "I pray that Peter's faith will not fail." Those words were uttered before the tragic night when Peter denied his Lord. That denial was Satan sifting him. But Jesus had prayed, "Father, though Peter must go through anguish and heartache, I pray that *when it happens*, his faith will hold firm, that You will take him through, and use it for good in his life."

All of our prayers ought to reflect this desire. Anything can happen in our lives—heartache, tragedy, joy, glory. But whatever happens, let us pray that it will deepen our faith, increase our love, open our blinded eyes to truth and reality, and result in spiritual maturity.

HANDLING YOUR SEX DRIVE

5

(4:1–8)

*I*F WE COULD CREATE a drug that would remove pleasure from the act of sex, we could change the whole moral climate of our country. We could reduce crime, bring an end to the scandal of divorce, eliminate teenage pregnancies, reduce the prison population, stop the sale of pornography, and decrease poverty.

But in doing so, we would also lose a special part of God's creation. We would forfeit some of the zest and spontaneity between the sexes, and life would become drab and dreary indeed. Since we obviously cannot make that drastic change, the only thing left for us to do is to learn how to handle our sexuality properly.

When I was a young man, nobody was teaching about sexuality. Back then, you grew up thinking that your body ended at the waist. If the word *sex* was ever used, especially in church, it was usually whispered. How people can read their Bibles every day and miss some of the great passages that teach openly about this subject, I don't know. But Paul had no such inhibitions in his first letter to the Thessalonian Christians. Along with instruction on the practical matters of learning how to get along with one another, how to handle the death of loved ones, and how to view God's apparent delay in the coming again of Jesus, he provided a treatise on how to handle one's sex drive.

PLEASING GOD

We may think of the ancients as very different from us, but they really were not. Those people who lived in the bustling seaport city of Thessalonica felt the same kind of pressures and drives we do. New Testament Thessalonica was rather like San Francisco—filled with business and commerce and the usual hustle and bustle of a large city, along with culture and beauty and art. But there was also degradation and sin, shame and sordidness. The Thessalonians were driven by the same forces that drive us. In the realism and wisdom of the Scriptures, therefore, the apostle taught them how to handle life in many practical areas.

First, he taught them that they "ought to live and to please God" (4:1 RSV). That is the number one subject in the curriculum of the Holy Spirit. The Christian's business is to live to please God. The word *ought*, which is made up of an elision of the two English words *owe it*, reflects that priority. We owe it to God to please Him! Paul tells us why, here and in other passages. "He died for all, that those who live should no longer live for themselves but for him who died for them and was raised again" (2 Cor. 5:15).

The great truth that every Christian must learn, says the apostle, is that "you are not your own." We no longer belong to ourselves. We cannot let our own desires take priority in life. Rather, we "are bought at a price" (1 Cor. 6:19–20). Jesus died on our behalf, in our place. You deserved that death; I deserved it. But He paid the penalty Himself. Now we belong to Him. He has invaded our being by the Holy Spirit, and the purpose of our lives has been dramatically transformed. We are to live no longer for ourselves but for Him who died for us and was raised again from the dead.

Every appeal to the Christian in the New Testament is made on that basis, and that is why Paul put it first here. The Christian "ought to live and to please God." As someone has well said, "The main thing is to see that the main thing remains the main thing." We ought to remind ourselves every day that our business is not to do what we want done but to please the Lord, who has redeemed us at such fearful cost.

Next, Paul taught the Thessalonians "how to live in order to please God." Notice the word *how*. It is significant that Paul did not merely teach these early Christians *what* they ought to do, but *how* to do it, especially in the area of handling sexuality.

Furthermore, Paul exhorted them to do these things (follow his instructions) "more and more." The Christian life is one of growth. There is progress to be made. A wider realm of application ought to be visible in our lives. All of us were disturbed about some aspect of our lives when we came to Christ. Perhaps it was our sex life. It may have been a deep sense of inferiority, or of shame and anger because we were unable to be what we ought to be. We came to Christ because we needed help. But we do not surrender just that one area of our life to Him; every aspect of our life is to be His to control.

The apostle reminds the Thessalonians of the clear instructions he gave on how to live to please God. Notice these are given "by the authority of the Lord Jesus." In other words, this is not just Paul's advice as a religious leader. These are the words and desires of our Lord—Jesus Himself. "It is God's will," says Paul, "that you should be sanctified."

Unfortunately, the word *sanctification* leads to confusion for many people.

Some think of it as a kind of religious sheep-dip they are put through: a once-for-all experience of cleansing and commitment. Once they have been dipped, they think everything is fine.

Others see sanctification as an extraction process. God uses a kind of supernatural magnet to extract all sin, and from that moment on they will have no trouble pleasing Him. Some people actually believe they have not sinned for years. Obviously, nobody has told them the truth yet. A little deeper investigation would reveal how wrong they are.

Actually, the word *sanctification* is almost the same as the word that is translated *holiness* in this passage; it comes from the same root. But many are confused about holiness, too. Many people think of holiness as "grimness." These kind of "holy" people look like they've been soaked in embalming fluid. They are dour and dull; they frown on anything that is fun or pleasurable. But that is not holiness.

The Old Testament speaks about "the beauty of holiness," the inner attractiveness that is apparent when someone begins to function inwardly as he or she was intended to function. What this says is that God is designing beautiful people! Not merely outwardly beautiful people like those we see on television, but inwardly beautiful people. People who are admirable, trustworthy, strong, loving, and compassionate—people who are whole. In fact, the word *wholeness* derives from the same root as *holiness*. And that is His will for us.

Wholeness includes moral purity. "Avoid sexual immorality" (v. 3), says the apostle in the very next sentence. You cannot be a whole person if you indulge in sexual immorality. But words like *immorality* do not seem to register with many people.

Let us put it plainly: Morality means *no sexual wrongdoing*. It means no making out in the backseat of the car; no premarital sex (no fornication); no messing around with someone else's husband or wife (no extramarital sex); no homosexual sex (the Scripture is very clear on this issue in many places); no pornography (no standing in the newsstand at the airport and flipping through *Penthouse* or *Playboy* magazines and getting yourself turned on by looking at the pictures; that is sexual fantasy, and it is wrong). To "avoid sexual immorality" means to have none of these things going on in your life.

Why? *Because such actions destroy the wholeness that both you and God want.* There is nothing more beautiful than a young person who has his or her life in order. I am saddened when I see wonderful young men and women who have been reared in godly homes to reflect the moral beauty in their lives gradually begin to let their standards go when they get out into the world. Watch them for a year or two, and you see the hardness in their faces as they begin to lose the beauty of holiness/wholeness God has planned for them.

You may be thinking that moral purity in our day is impossible, or that it is too late for you; you have already messed up your life. The Word does not say we must never do these things; rather, the Word says, "Do them no longer." All of us have messed up in one way or another; we have destroyed the wholeness already. But the glory of the gospel is that in coming to Jesus, through His work on the cross in our behalf and His rising again from the dead, we have been given a new start. The past is wiped out and forgiven. We are restored. "I have espoused you [I have betrothed you] as a chaste virgin unto Christ" (2 Cor. 11:2 KJV), wrote Paul. Even though the Corinthians had already messed up their lives with many sexual sins, Paul assured them that in Christ they were as chaste as virgins.

And even if as a Christian you have fouled up, the Word of God says very clearly that you can be restored. If you acknowledge that you have done wrong and accept God's forgiveness through Christ, you are "a chaste virgin" again in Christ. What glorious good news!

ACHIEVING MORAL PURITY

In his instructions to the Christians in Thessalonica, Paul gave two steps toward achieving moral purity.

1. *Learn to control your own body.* In the Greek text, the word translated *body* is actually *vessel*, though it is clear from the context that Paul was talking about our bodies. They are the vessels, the "temple of the Holy Spirit" (1 Cor. 6:19).

But learning how to handle our bodies properly is not always easy. God gave our bodies to us; we did not design them ourselves. We would probably change a lot of things if it were up to us to recreate or even rearrange our bodies. Included in the gift of our bodies is a remarkable capacity to churn out certain hormones that pour into the bloodstream. These hormones have a profound effect upon the way our bodies function. At puberty, new hormones pour into the bloodstream and we experience sexual changes, along with powerful drives that almost seem to compel us to certain sexual activities. Society tells us that those urges are natural and therefore ought to be satisfied whenever opportunity affords. Worldlings argue that the sexual appetite should be satisfied just like hunger, thirst, exhaustion, or any other natural need. This argument says there is nothing wrong with the fulfilling of sexual desires.

Now they are right in saying that sex is a natural function, but what they are not saying, and what the Scriptures reveal, is that all natural functions need certain degrees of control. Take hunger, for instance. You do not eat anytime you feel like eating. You learn to control your appetite. The same applies to sleep. You do not go to sleep whenever you feel like it.

Control increases the enjoyment of a natural function. For example, you enjoy your food more if you do not eat between meals. When a flooding river is controlled by banks, its intensity is increased.

Many young people are discovering that in these days when moral restraints are removed from sexual practices, the result is a kind of listless flood in which one wades continually with no enjoyment whatsoever. But God has designed sex to be stimulating and arousing. That is why marriage constitutes a kind of channeled control for sex. There is ample provision made for the stream, but the limits increase the intensity and enjoyment. That is what God has in mind as part of the process of producing a whole person. Anything that tears down those boundaries destroys the strength and beauty of wholeness.

So Paul says that we are to learn how to control our bodies in holiness—wholeness—and honor. Control contributes to that sense of wholeness. You are to be in charge of your own body. You are not to be bound to it. You are not to be a slave to it.

THOSE THOU SHALT NOTS!

After Paul states the positive, he also gives the negative: *Don't give way to "passionate lust* like the heathen, who do not know God" (v. 5).

In order to learn control, we must avoid the slavery of lust.

A young man told me once: "I got into messing around sexually right out of high school, and I have been doing it ever since. In fact, I would have to say that I am nothing but a male whore!" He meant that he was a slave to lust. He had allowed his sexuality to rage out of control until it possessed his life and he was no longer a free person. That is what Christians must avoid. Paul taught the Thessalonian believers not to give in to the sexual pressures of their lustful city. They were to restrain themselves and learn how to handle their bodies rightly and thus reflect the beauty, orderliness, and glory of a life that was whole.

Secondly, he said: *"no one should wrong his brother or take advantage of him"* (v. 6). Let me put it plainly: this means no adultery; no haunting the houses of prostitution; no sexual involvement with anyone but your marriage partner; no carrying on affairs with your neighbor's wife or husband. Such behavior wrongs others. It steals their property and destroys their rights. The tenth commandment says, "You shall not covet your neighbor's wife, or his manservant or maidservant, his ox or donkey, or anything that belongs to your neighbor" (Ex. 20:17). That perhaps is what some of the Thessalonians were doing, and their conduct had not only destroyed the wholeness of their own lives, but had also hurt others. In counseling, pastors hear seemingly endless stories of damaged families, of children's lives being ruined by the adulterous affairs of their parents. Enormous misery and heartache follow the passions of adultery and sexual affairs.

Paul says there is a dreadful price to pay for all this. "The Lord will punish men for all such sins, as we have already told you and warned you" (v. 6). God so loves His creation and so longs to see beautiful, whole people emerging from it that He will take drastic action when people violate His will. Silently, His judgment falls. Believer and unbeliever alike cannot escape the painful results of sinful choices. That is the law of inevitable consequences. If we choose to sin, there will be evil results. We cannot avoid them. We can be forgiven, but that does not change the results. Forgiveness restores the broken relationship and gives us strength to walk on in freedom in the future, but it does not change or eliminate the hurt of the past.

Every believer must face that unalterable fact. Throughout the Old Testament God sought to impart to Israel the fact that if they violated His laws, if they refused to hear His Word, ugly and terrible things would happen to them. Listen to these words from Deuteronomy 31 where God is speaking to Israel about their disobedience: "On that day I will become angry with them and forsake them; I will hide my face from them and they will be destroyed. Many disasters and difficulties will come upon them, and on that day they will ask, 'Have not these disasters come upon us because our God is not with us?'" (v. 17). That discipline took the form of famine, war, and disease. And the final judgment would be a breakup of families: "Your sons and your daughters will be given to another nation, and you will wear out your eyes watching for them day after day, powerless to lift a hand" (Ex. 28:32).

Isn't that what has happened here in the United States, where one-half of all children today live with single parents?

Families have been broken and children parceled out to strangers.

The final step, God said, would be "a despairing soul" (28:65), that awful depression of spirit that makes one want to commit suicide rather than to go on living. As a faithful father, Paul solemnly forewarned the Thessalonians that this would happen. God's standards cannot be violated. He has ways of bringing His judgments to pass, and nobody can evade them.

LOVE WARNS

The apostle recaps this teaching in two wonderful verses: "For God has not called us for uncleanness, but in holiness [wholeness]. Therefore whoever disregards this, disregards not man but God, who gives his Holy Spirit to you" (1 Thess. 4:7–8).

These solemn words of warning are set against the background of God's yearning for a whole person. God has called us to wholeness. That is what He can create if we obey what He says. If we disregard His instructions, says Paul, we are not only turning our backs on what He has said, but on God Himself and His supply of power to enable us to carry out His instructions.

In the campaign against drug abuse we are being told that what we need to teach children is to "just say no." But those who are already addicted to drugs tell us that is difficult to do. When the terrible passion for a drug is throbbing through every vessel of the body, it is very hard to "just say no." The will is not strong enough, and they give in again and again. Now God knows that. He knows how we function. That is why He has provided a new resource for believers, the Holy Spirit. Remember the wonderful promise of Ephesians 3:20: "Now to him who is able to do im-measurably more than all we ask or imagine, *according to his power that is at work within us.*"

If we give the excuse that we cannot do what God commands, we deny that we have been provided with an extra resource. We may need to exercise our will to "just say no," but then we must immediately cast ourselves upon the Spirit of God within us—the Lord Jesus made available by the Spirit. Resting upon that presence, we must turn and walk away. We can do it. We have the power. Millions can testify that what they could not do by their own will they were able to do by relying on the power of God.

We live in an immoral world. Young people are under pressure I never faced as a young man. But God has told us we can live a holy life. The following words of a great hymn eloquently express the rallying call we need to hear today:

> *Rise up, O men of God!*
> *Have done with lesser things;*
> *Give heart and soul and mind and strength*
> *To serve the King of kings.*
>
> *Lift high the cross of Christ!*
> *Tread where His feet have trod;*
> *As brothers of the Son of Man,*
> *Rise up, O men of God!*

God wants a community of beautiful people whose lives are under control and maintained by the Holy Spirit. Such a people will constitute an island of refuge and resource for the drifting multitudes who are still enslaved by their own passions and desires.

COMFORT AT THE GRAVE | 6

(4:9–18)

WE NEVER KNOW what circumstances we will face tomorrow. But today comes before tomorrow, and that is where we must live. We cannot live tomorrow, but we can live today. This is the issue that was troubling the Thessalonian Christians. They were looking toward tomorrow but wondering what to do today. The apostle Paul's advice to them in his first letter was, as usual, very practical.

LIVING TODAY

When confronted with the question of how to live in the present moment, Paul's excellent advice was: "Stay loving and keep working" (4:9–12).

First, keep on loving! Keep your attitude toward others warm and gracious. Watch how you speak. If you offend someone, correct it. When I spoke at our New Year's Eve service a few years ago, I said an ungracious word to a man who was trying to help me adjust the microphone. Afterward I had to go to him and apologize and ask his forgiveness. We must keep loving and forgiving one another. We must refrain from being bitter, resentful, sarcastic, or critical.

Keep Loving

Paul told the Thessalonians that he did not need to teach them how to love one another. His amazing claim was that God through His Holy Spirit would teach them. "God has poured out his love into our hearts by the Holy Spirit, whom he has given us," said the apostle in Romans 5:5. If we welcome that love of the Spirit, we will be able to manifest love toward others. If we choose to be bitter, of course, then love will not be manifested. But if we reject the caustic word, the sharp attitude, then we can show kindness, mercy, and grace. The Holy Spirit gives believers a new capacity to love that the worldling does not possess.

On the other hand, many people make the mistake of believing that Christians will immediately *feel* loving. Christians feel the same way non-Christians do. We often feel angry, put upon, resentful, and repulsed. Here is how one Christian writer described it:

> Loving people is about the most difficult thing that some of us do. We can be patient with people and even just and charitable, but how are we supposed to conjure up in our hearts that warm effervescent sentiment of good will which the New Testament calls love? Some people are so miserably unlovable. That odorous person

with the nasty cough who sat next to you in the train
shoving his newspaper into your face. Those crude louts
in the neighborhood with the barking dog. That smooth
liar who took you in so completely last week. By what
magic are you supposed to feel toward these people
anything but revulsion, distrust and resentment, and a
justified desire to have nothing to do with them?

Though this attitude is understandable at times, the
wonderful good news is that we do not have to act on our
feelings. We do not have to regard others as rivals or enemies.
We can look upon them as victims in need of sympathy and
help. Then, by drawing on the grace God has given us, we
can begin to act lovingly. Love is a decision we make to draw
on Another's strength. That is why the apostle told the Thessalonians to love each other and to "do so more and more."

Stay Busy

Second, the apostle told the Thessalonian Christians to
keep their hands busy with profitable labor. People under
stress need to remain busy. They should not dwell on their
own needs and feel sorry for themselves. It is clear from
Paul's description that some believers had stopped working
because they thought the end of the age and the coming of
the Lord was at hand. As days and weeks went by and the
Lord did not come, they ran out of food and would have
starved if Christian friends and neighbors had not come to
their aid. Thus, they had become a burden to others.

True faith in Christ, even faith in the second coming of
Jesus, does not produce fanaticism. It does not encourage
people to abandon everything to wait for Jesus' coming. We
need to recall that one of the last words of our Lord to His
disciples was, "Occupy till I come" (Luke 19:13 KJV). Even He

did not know what day that would be. Mark records that the disciples asked Him, "What day and hour will you return?" And Jesus replied, "I do not know. Only the Father knows that." As a man, He did not know the time of His return. He could have known if He had chosen to, but He did not know because He had left that in the Father's hands. The Christians in Thessalonica were making fools of themselves by stressing the immediacy of the coming of the Lord to such a degree that they had stopped working. That is why the apostle told them to keep busy.

In 1846, a man named William Miller predicted that Jesus was coming at a certain day and hour. A group of his followers quit their jobs, sold their possessions, and went out on a hilltop to wait for the Lord to appear. There was tremendous expectancy on their part, but, of course, Jesus did not come. To onlookers they appeared ridiculous because of this extreme action. The apostle Paul corrects that kind of thinking in words to this effect: "Make it your ambition to lead a quiet life, to mind your own business and to work with your hands, just as we told you, so that your daily life may win the respect of outsiders and so that you will not be dependent on anybody" (v. 11–12).

LOOKING FOR TOMORROW

Twice in this passage Paul uses a term for death that likens it to sleep: "God will bring with Jesus those who have fallen asleep" (v. 14). That term, by the way, is never used in the New Testament of anyone but believers. It never says of a non-believer's death that he "fell asleep." Jesus declared of Jairus' daughter who had died, "She is not dead but asleep" (Matt. 9:24). What a wonderful lesson. Death for the believer, according to the Scriptures, is nothing more than sleep. And when your loved ones fall asleep at night, you do not run to the phone and dial 911 for emergency service. You know that they are quietly resting, that they will awaken again, and that you will have contact with them soon. It is an encouraging word for those who are facing the death of someone dear.

The question the Thessalonian believers were asking was, "Will we see our loved ones again?" They were expecting the Lord to return any day. They felt their loved ones who had died would not be resurrected until the final resurrection at the end of time. They would not see them again until that far-off event. In this, they were like the sister of Lazarus in the gospel of John. Jesus said to Martha, "Your brother will rise again." Martha replied, "I know he will rise again in the resurrection at the last day" (John 11:23–24). She imagined that Jesus was referring to the Old Testament teaching of the resurrection of all the dead, believers and unbelievers alike, in the last day. But Jesus intended to do something about Lazarus right then and there. As we know from that narrative, He did raise Lazarus from the dead on that very occasion. Like Martha, the Thessalonians did not understand. They thought it would be a long time before they saw their loved ones again. We can best understand this account if we remember five simple steps:

1. *The Thessalonians had clearly been expecting Jesus to return before any of them died.* His return was a moment-by-moment expectancy in the early church. First-century Christians believed the Lord was coming at any moment. In the first chapter of this letter Paul commends the Thessalonians for waiting for God's Son from heaven. That is what they were looking for. Jesus' own words suggest that this would be the case. All His statements about His return were addressed to people still alive, and He spoke as though they

would still be alive when He returned. To His disciples He said, "Watch, because you do not know the day or the hour" (Matt. 25:13). He used such terms as "be not deceived" (Luke 21:8 KJV), and "the Son of Man will come at an hour when you do not expect him" (Matt. 24:44). There is no mention of the impact of His coming upon those who had already died.

2. *The Thessalonians, like many of us today, were projecting the sequences of time into eternity.* We all struggle with the concept of eternity. We tend to think of it as time going on endlessly; that, as is the case here on earth, we must wait for certain events that are yet future. That is how it will be in heaven, we feel, despite the fact that the Word of God seeks to demonstrate that time and eternity are two different things. Time has sequences: past, present, and future. But eternity has only one dimension: it is present, now. We struggle with that concept, as did the Thessalonians.

Here we are all locked into a segment of time together. If we are in the same location, we are all feeling the same temperature, the same barometric pressure. But that is true only of our bodies; it says nothing about where our minds are at any given moment. Minds are not limited to space or time or sequence. They can go anywhere and experience anything at any time. Eternity is much more like that. That is why we have great difficulty understanding these prophetic passages in terms of time when they are really eternal events.

Although I believe Paul knew the difference between time and eternity, he reassured the Thessalonians without becoming abstruse or pedantic, explaining that the living and the dead would be together when our Lord returns. That is the point at issue. He says, in effect, "Yes, you will see your loved ones immediately when the Lord returns. Whether you join that event when you die, or whether the Lord comes while you are yet alive, your loved ones will be with Him."

3. *The Thessalonians gained new insight about Jesus' second coming "according to the Lord's own word."* I take those words to mean that this is something Paul had not taught them when he was in Thessalonica. He had taught them about Jesus' death and resurrection and how that would affect them, but now he provided further truth. "We who are alive, who are left till the coming of the Lord, will certainly not precede those who have fallen asleep" (v. 15). "Don't worry," Paul reassured them. "You will find your loved ones again when the Lord returns. We will all be together." This is new revelation, given now "by the word of the Lord."

4. *The Thessalonians learned the details of the Second Coming—the sequence of events as they will occur.* Many people, including certain notable Bible scholars, are confused on this because they regard the coming of the Lord as a single event, an immediate and once-for-all appearing. But if we carefully study the Scriptures, we find that the coming of the Lord is a series of events. This series has a dramatic beginning: "The Lord himself will come down from heaven" to take His saints, living and dead, to be with Him (v. 16). And it has an even more dramatic ending when He will manifest Himself to the entire world: "They will see the Son of Man coming on the clouds of the sky, with power and great glory" (Matt. 24:30). These are two separate events. In between is a period of time during which Jesus is present on the earth, though not always visible.

That is what Scripture calls the "presence," which is the Greek word *parousia*.[1] I personally believe *presence* is a better translation than *coming*. When Scripture talks about the com-

---

[1]See Appendix for an explanation of the author's interpretation of *parousia*.

ing of the Lord, it sometimes looks at the beginning of that series, sometimes at the end of it, and sometimes, as in the book of Revelation, at what is going on in the time between. We must train ourselves to think in those terms. The *parousia* of Jesus is a series of events. Daniel, the Old Testament prophet, said that it would be a week of years—that is, seven years in duration. One event takes place at the beginning; another event takes place at the end. In between, the Lord will be present on the earth behind the scenes, as it were, very much as He was in the days after His resurrection.

For forty days Jesus was here on earth. He appeared to the disciples in Jerusalem and in Galilee. People heard reports that He was around, but nobody could find Him except when He chose to be seen. That is the same condition that will prevail on earth during this time of the coming of the Lord. If we understand that, it will help us greatly to comprehend what is described in this passage.

SOUNDS OF HIS COMING

The apostle connected three sounds with this initial appearing of Jesus.

First, he said, "The Lord himself will come down from heaven, with a *loud command*." It always warms my heart to remember that it is the Lord Himself who will come; He is not going to send Michael, the archangel, or Gabriel or anyone else. And at that "loud command" . . . "all who are in their graves will hear his voice and come out" (John 5:28).

Jesus had once stood before the tomb of Lazarus and cried with a loud voice, "Lazarus, come forth," and to the amazement of the crowd the dead man appeared in the doorway, still wrapped in his grave clothes. As many commentators have pointed out, if Jesus had not called the name "Lazarus," He would have emptied the graveyard! But the hour is coming when all the dead shall hear the voice of the Son of God and come forth! That is what Paul is talking about here. The cry of command will be addressed to the dead, to those in the graves.

The second sound is *"the voice of the archangel"* (v. 16). The only angel in the Bible called an archangel is Michael. Though Gabriel is a great angel, he is never referred to as an archangel. In the first two verses of Daniel 12 we read that an angel said to Daniel, "At that time Michael, the great prince who protects your people [Israel] will arise"; Michael is always connected with Israel. Michael shall stand up and then there shall be a resurrection; those who are in the tombs will come forth, Daniel was told. Also, the living nation of Israel will be summoned to a new relationship with God. Details of this event concern the 144,000 Israelites, twelve thousand from each of the twelve tribes of Israel, who are described in Revelation 7 and 14. These will be called to follow Jesus wherever He goes during the time of His presence on earth. He will be invisible to the world but visible to them. That all begins when Jesus returns for His church and the archangel calls Israel into a new relationship with the Lord.

The third sound is *"the trumpet call of God"* such as was heard at Mount Sinai when the Law was given. At that time the trumpet sounded so loudly that the people cried out to Moses and trembled with fear. I do not think the whole world will hear this call. In 1 Corinthians 15, the great resurrection chapter, Paul says, "Listen, I tell you a mystery: We will not all sleep [i.e., not all believers will go to heaven by death], but we will all be changed—in a flash, in the twinkling of an eye, *at the last trumpet"* (15:51–52). This verse speaks of those saints who will be alive when Christ returns. We are not all going to die; but the important thing is that "we will all be changed." Although inaudible to the world, when that trumpet call reaches the ears of living believers, they will be changed and caught up to be with the Lord.

A COMFORTING WORD

The comforting hope is that we shall all be together as the great family of God, "with the Lord forever" (1 Thess. 4:17). Whatever the church does from that point on, it will be done with the Lord.

As I have suggested, I believe He will actually remain on earth, behind the scenes, directing the events described in the dramatic portrayal of the book of Revelation. The church will be with Him, invisibly participating in directing the course of the Great Tribulation, but not going through it because we are no longer living on earth; we are transformed saints affecting the events on earth. The critical point Paul stresses is that we shall see Jesus face to face. That has always been a source of great comfort to believers through the centuries.

One Christmas I received a beautiful painting of a mountain and lake in Glacier Park, Montana. I had stood by that lake and looked at that mountain, and the painting brought back to me the majesty and beauty of the scene. I remember thinking, "I wish I could live here and look at this every morning."

Last year I stood on the edge of a cliff in Mendocino County, looking out over the great breakers of the Pacific dashing up one hundred feet or more into the air. It was a spectacle of awesome power. I thought how great it would be to live here all the time.

If the beauty of creation makes us shiver with anticipation, what will it be like to behold the Creator face-to-face? If we tingle at the shadow, what will it be to see the Substance Himself? If we revel in nature's masterpieces, what will it mean to be face-to-face with the Artist Himself?

Samuel Rutherford was one of the Scottish Covenanters of the seventeenth century who served the Lord during times of persecution in Scotland. Elizabeth Clephane took some phrases from Rutherford's beautiful letters and put them together in one of the most popular hymns of the nineteenth century. It was D. L. Moody's favorite hymn, and it has always been a great favorite of mine.

> *The sands of time are sinking,*
> *The dawn of heaven breaks;*
> *The summer morn I've sighed for—*
> *The fair, sweet morn awakes:*
> *Dark, dark hath been the midnight,*
> *But dayspring is at hand,*
> *And glory, glory dwelleth*
> *In Immanuel's land.*
>
> *O Christ, He is the fountain,*
> *The deep, sweet well of love!*
> *The streams on earth I've tasted*
> *More deep I'll drink above:*
> *There to an ocean fullness*
> *His mercy doth expand,*
> *And glory, glory dwelleth*
> *In Immanuel's land.*

> *The Bride eyes not her garment,*
> *But her dear Bridegroom's face;*
> *I will not gaze at glory*
> *But on my King of grace.*
> *Not at the crown He giveth*
> *But on His pierced hand:*
> *The Lamb is all the glory*
> *Of Immanuel's land.*

What a marvelous hope we have! When we face the thought of our own death, or when we stand at the grave of a loved one, we are comforted indeed by this tremendous vision of the tomorrow that awaits God's own. That is the apostle's purpose in giving this revelation. Let us revel in it.

THE FATE OF THE EARTH

7

(5:1–11)

*H*AVING BEEN IN THE Middle East where I was able to observe personally many of the turbulent currents that are challenging the peace of the world in that area, I realize why people are concerned about the fate of the earth. The title of this chapter is borrowed from a book by Jonathan Schell. Published in 1982, it describes in chilling detail what would happen if this country went through a nuclear war. It is a grim and pessimistic account that offers little hope if such a holocaust should occur. President Jimmy Carter's remarks in his farewell address capture the essence of it: "The survivors, if any, would live in despair amid the poisoned ruins of a civilization that had committed suicide."

The fifth chapter of 1 Thessalonians also deals with the fate of the earth, but from God's point of view. Unlike the pessimism of the secular prophets, there is a strong note of hope amid the darkness and judgment predicted. In the closing verses of chapter 4, dealing with the second coming (or *parousia*) of Christ, we learned that Christians are not waiting for the judgments and wrath of God but for the coming of the Son of God, either at their own death or when He breaks into time in the event described in verses 16–18.

Ignoring the chapter division inserted by some unnamed scribe, the thought continues into chapter 5 with the transition of the conjunction *but* (RSV). Whenever we come upon the word *but* in the Scriptures, we can be sure we are turning a corner; the same subject will be covered, but from a different perspective and direction.

THE TIMES AND THE SEASONS

The phrase "times and dates" indicates that the apostle is coming to grips with the question of the time of the Lord's return. All of us seem to want to circle a date on the calendar, but Paul taught the Thessalonians that they did not need to know the precise date. "Now, brothers, about times and dates," he said, "we do not need to write to you" (5:1). He knew they had already been reading in the Old Testament about the Day of the Lord; the description and characteristics of that day were familiar to them.

Remember, the "day" of the Lord is not a twenty-four-hour day; it is an extended length of time, covering a number of events over a period of probably seven years. The whole period is called the *parousia* or the "presence" of Christ. As I understand Scripture, when Christ returns He will remain on earth for this period. Thus, the "day of the Lord" covers a series of events, perhaps even extending into the millennium, the thousand-year reign of Christ that follows. Actually, the phrase "day of the Lord" refers to any period of time when God acts directly and unmistakably in human affairs. It may be in blessing, as in the pouring out of the Holy Spirit on the Day of Pentecost, or it may be in judgment. Or it may be that the same event will be a judgment to some people and a blessing to others.

Jesus said much the same thing. During that mysterious period of time after He had risen from the dead and appeared to His disciples, then disappeared again, they asked Him, "Lord, are you at this time going to restore the kingdom to Israel?" In other words, they were asking, "Is this the time when You will fulfill the predictions of the prophets that Israel will be the chief of the nations and the Messiah will reign personally upon the earth?"

His remarkable answer to their question was: "It is not for you to know the times or dates [the same phrase as here] the Father has set by his own authority" (Acts 1:7). In other words, only the Father knew the answer to their question. Then Jesus went on to outline the program that would affect them: "But you will receive power when the Holy Spirit comes on you; and you will be my witnesses in Jerusalem, and in all Judea and Samaria, and to the ends of the earth" (v. 8).

We must understand that though we cannot name the precise date when the Lord will appear and begin the Day of the Lord, there are three characteristics of that day that we will be able to recognize.

THE DAY OF THE LORD

The first characteristic of the Day of the Lord, said Paul to the Thessalonians, is that *it will come stealthily.* It will come "like a thief in the night" (v. 2). I recall hearing of an incident where an entire family was sleeping upstairs one night when someone entered their home and stole several items of value; the thief came and left without their knowing it. That is the way a professional thief operates. He enters silently and unobtrusively and does his work. That, said Paul, is the way the Lord will come.

We hear these days about the new Stealth bomber, which the Air Force has developed. The plane is designed in such a way that it cannot be detected by radar. It can come upon an enemy unexpectedly, without warning. The Lord will come stealthily, said Paul, at a time when "peace and safety" seem to prevail, when nothing out of the ordinary is expected. That is how the Day of the Lord begins.

This is not just the apostle Paul's idea. Jesus had confirmed this truth earlier when he said that the Day of the Lord would come when life seemed to be proceeding normally. People will be eating, drinking, and marrying when suddenly the destructive judgment of God will fall (Luke 17: 26–27). And that judgment is introduced, as Jesus pointed out very clearly, by the removal of the family of God from the earth: *"the day Noah entered the ark. Then the flood came and destroyed them all"* (v. 27).

Jesus did not stop there, however. He went on to say, "It was the same in the days of Lot. People were eating and drinking, buying and selling, planting and building [normal, everyday activities]. But the day Lot left Sodom, fire and sulfur rained down from heaven and destroyed them all. It will be just like this on the day the Son of man is revealed" (vv. 28–29).

Notice how clearly our Lord indicates in both of the examples He uses that there will first be a quiet disappearance of the family of God. Like a thief at work, silently and stealthily, the treasure will be taken away. Then the judgment will come.

In Matthew 24, the famous Olivet discourse, Jesus mentions that of two men working in the field, one will be taken and the other left. Of two women grinding at the mill, one is taken and one is left.

A parallel passage in Luke says that two men will be asleep in one bed, and one will be taken and the other left. The examples occur during both day (working in the fields) and night (sleeping in bed). This indicates that this selective removal will happen simultaneously all over the earth. When it is day in one country and night in another, some will be taken and others left.

Jesus then adds a clear and unmistakable warning to be watchful and ready, "because the Son of Man will come at an hour when you do not expect him" (Matt. 24:44). So Scripture teaches that the Day of the Lord will begin with the removal of God's people.

WHEN JUDGMENT COMES

The Day of the Lord will also come suddenly, with terrible and destructive judgment.

The Thessalonian Christians were thoroughly familiar with the stark and dramatic prophecies of Joel, Isaiah, and Zephaniah: The Day of the Lord would be "a day of darkness and gloom, a day of clouds and blackness" (Joel 2:2). "The sky trembles, the sun and the moon are darkened, and the stars no longer shine" (vv. 10–11). "They will flee . . . from the splendor of his majesty, when he rises to shake the earth" (Isa. 2:21). "A day of wrath . . . a day of distress and anguish, a day of trouble and ruin, a day of darkness and gloom" (Zeph. 1:15).

All this is summed up in the words Jesus uttered on the Mount of Olives: "For then there will be great distress, unequaled from the beginning of the world until now—and never to be equaled again" (Matt. 24:21).

These are hard passages to preach from, hard passages to read, but they represent reality. The one thing we must do is to face exactly what God says is going to happen. Here is indeed the fate of the earth!

AN INESCAPABLE FACT

The Day of the Lord is inevitable. "They will not escape," says the apostle Paul, who likens that day to a woman in labor, whose time has come to give birth.

When our first daughter was born, we were living in a trailer on the campus of Dallas Theological Seminary. At two o'clock one morning, my wife indicated that the baby was coming. I put her in our old clunker of a car, which promptly refused to start. We had to enlist the aid of the garbage collectors, who were doing their rounds, to push the car and get it started. By the time we arrived at the hospital, the baby was well on its way! When a woman is ready to give birth, she can't change her mind. Ready or not, the baby is coming.

It is that inevitability that the apostle is highlighting. The world cannot escape the terrible judgments of God. And the only way we can handle this sobering thought is to find the means of escape provided in Jesus Christ our Lord.

In this connection, the words of C. S. Lewis are particularly apt:

God is going to invade this earth in force, but what is
the good of saying you are on his side then when you
see the whole natural universe melting away like a
dream and something else, something it never entered
your head to conceive, comes crashing in; something so
beautiful to some of us and so terrible to others that
none of us will have any choice left? For this time it will
be God without disguise; something so overwhelming
that it will strike either irresistible love or irresistible
horror into every creature. It will be too late then to
choose your side. There is no use saying you choose to
lie down when it has become impossible to stand up.
That will not be the time for choosing. It will be the time
when we discover which side we have really chosen
whether we realized it before or not. Now, today, this
moment is our chance to choose the right side. God is
holding back to give us that chance. It will not last
forever. We must take it or leave it.

It is vital that we understand that God's delay of this
event is for the purpose of giving people a chance to escape—
to see what is happening in their lives and to choose the
redemption that is in Christ Jesus our Lord.

HOW TO ESCAPE THE COMING JUDGMENT

After this terrible picture of gloom and darkness, verse
4 turns another corner. It too begins with the word *but*. "But
you, brothers, are not in darkness, so that this day should
surprise you like a thief. You are all sons of the light and sons
of the day. We do not belong to the night or to the darkness."
"You shouldn't be caught by surprise," Paul was
saying. "There is good news for all believers. We have been

enlightened about the escape route—our Lord Jesus Christ, who died for us" (v. 4–10). Our only hope, then, is to turn to the Lord and rely upon His death and resurrection. That is what Paul calls becoming a child of light and not of darkness. In his letter to the Colossians, he echoes this truth: "He has rescued us from the dominions of darkness and brought us into the kingdom of the Son he loves" (1:13).

Also we have been given knowledge and truth. The Word of God tells us exactly what will happen and confirms it by the prophecies that have been fulfilled through the centuries. In this connection I often think of that wonderful promise in the third chapter of Revelation, given to the church of Philadelphia: "Since you have kept my command to endure patiently [i.e., you have begun to run your life according to my Word], I will also keep you from the hour of trial that is going to come upon the whole world to test those who live on the earth" (v. 10).

For this reason Paul could say here: "God did not appoint us to suffer wrath" (1 Thess. 5:9). If we trust in the Lord Jesus, if we have been born again by the Spirit, if we believe His Word and are growing by it, we are not destined for wrath but are guaranteed an escape from this terrible time of judgment, just as Noah and Lot escaped the judgments that fell in their day.

THE PROMISE OF FOREVER

Not only will believers be spared that time of judgment, but "whether we are awake or asleep," we who are His are saved to "live together with him." The closing words of chapter 4 are equally triumphant: "So we will always be with the Lord forever" (4:17).

In his second letter, the apostle Peter (2 Peter 1:16–18) links this truth to Jesus' transfiguration. Here Peter refers to the time when he, James, and John were invited by the Lord to accompany Him to a mountaintop to pray.

A spur of Mount Hermon, which bears the name Mount Mizar, fits the description of the place where Jesus was transfigured. There, on that "very high mountain" in the north of Israel, Jesus was transformed so that His garments glowed like the sun. Peter, James, and John saw Him talking there with Moses and Elijah. "We did not follow cleverly invented stories when we told you about the power and *coming* of our Lord Jesus Christ [that is the word *parousia*, the coming, the presence], but we were eyewitnesses of his majesty" (v. 16). Peter says that God, in His inimitable teaching style, was previewing the *parousia* of the Lord through this transfiguration experience; that Jesus would come again and be related to people as He related to those who were with Him on the mountain that day.

Peter goes on to say: "For he received honor and glory from God the Father when the voice came to him from the Majestic Glory, saying, 'This is my Son, whom I love; with him I am well pleased.' We ourselves heard this voice that came from heaven when we were with him on the sacred mountain" (vv. 17–18). This is God's way of teaching us His relationship to believers in that day.

Hundreds of years earlier Moses had stood on Mount Nebo looking out over the Promised Land that he was forbidden to enter because of his own failure at a certain point in the wilderness journey. Moses died on that mountaintop and was buried by God; no one knows where. But now he was a resurrected saint, appearing on the Mount of Transfiguration with Jesus and Elijah, another Old Testament believer who never died but was translated.

So at the second coming of our Lord (the parousia) those who are raised from the dead will join with those who are alive and remain—translated, as Paul puts it in 1 Corinthians 15: "We will not all sleep, but we will all be changed—in a flash, in the twinkling of an eye" (vv. 51–52). Moses and Elijah represent those two kinds of saints: Moses, having died; Elijah, being caught up alive. With them are three ordinary mortals—Peter, James, and John. So during the Tribulation period (and during the Millennium that follows) resurrected saints and translated saints will exist with mortal human beings upon the earth. This transfiguration scene previews that event. And in the center, as the focus of all attention, is the risen, glorified, transfigured Lord Himself.

STAYING AWAKE UNTIL HE COMES

This is God's picture of the fate of the earth. As we learn what is coming in world affairs, we can understand that the hope of the believer is to be with Christ. We have given our hearts to Him already, and He will claim us, body, soul, and spirit, on that day.

What should be the result in our lives? Paul gives some down-to-earth advice on how to live in this present day.

Wake Up!

The apostle stirs us from our apathy and from fantasies and dreams such as the world dreams. Our purpose for living is not to gain wealth and fame, to be self-centered, but to use our abilities and time to fulfill the will of God. We are to find the adventure, excitement, and drama inherent in His call rather than to waste time in self-indulgence. "Be alert,"

92 Waiting for the Second Coming

warns the apostle (v. 6). "Do not lose sight of reality. This is the hour when God is about to move on earth again. Snap out of your lethargy and tune in to His voice."

Get Serious!

When Paul suggests that we "be self-controlled," he is not saying we must be grim and humorless, that we must forget all rest and recreation. He is simply urging us to take life more seriously. Do not spend your time amusing yourself constantly. As the apostle puts it in Ephesians 5:15–16: "Be wise . . . making the most of every opportunity, because the days are evil." Take advantage of the contacts you have with people to help them, to reach out to them. Love, support, encourage, and minister to one another.

Some time ago our church staff boarded a plane in Chicago for the final leg of a return trip from Israel. It was late at night, and there was no dinner to be served, so the flight attendants had time to talk with the passengers. Several of our young pastors gathered in the back of the plane and began to talk with some of the attendants about the Lord. One of them received the Lord and promised to be in our church within the next few days; another accepted a Bible. These young women were spiritually hungry and eager to listen.

Even though the pastors had been flying for thirteen hours and had planned to catch up on their sleep from Chicago to San Francisco, they were so caught up in the excitement of witnessing that they didn't sleep a wink. They felt the thrill of fulfillment in reaching out to these hungry hearts with the living Bread.

So the apostle Paul tells us to use our opportunities to spread the good news. Wake up to the opportunity of the day.

And finally, we are to "encourage one another and build each other up" (1 Thess. 5:11). It is so easy to lose sight of God's perspective. In a world that shoves God off to the side and is forever caught up in the things of the moment, it is easy to think that life ought always to be beautiful and wonderful. It is so easy to slip into the worldly attitude that protests in the face of trial, "Why me? What have I done to deserve this?"

We need to encourage one another and help one another to understand that no job is insignificant when done "as unto the Lord." No task is meaningless when it involves reaching out in love to someone else. God is not forgetful of our labors of love, the apostle tells us.

I occasionally receive encouraging letters saying how much my teaching has meant to someone. What a lift that gives to my spirit! That is what we ought to be doing for one another. As Paul says: "Build each other up, just as in fact you are doing."

LIVING CHRISTIANLY | 8

(5:12–28)

ONCE I HEARD a man say, "The most important thing in learning to relate to others is personal honesty. Once you learn to fake that," he added, "everything else is easy!" Many people, unfortunately, seem to follow that philosophy. As a result, we are seeing not only the moral collapse of our leaders, but a low level of ethical behavior on the part of many Christians.

I do not understand what has happened to the Christian community in this regard. Believers who go to church regularly and profess to believe the Bible seem to be going along with practices of the world around them, apparently unaware or unconcerned that what they are doing is unbiblical and sinful. They lie without hesitation. They don't pay their bills. They cheat on their taxes. They ignore needy people. They fail to keep appointments. They freeload shamelessly. They lose their tempers. They grow critical and caustic. They desert their mates. If the apostle Paul were here, he would be very concerned about this. To him, the mark of true Christian faith was its ability to change everything—to affect every area of life. A Christian may no longer act as he or she did before coming to Christ. This is very clear in the letters of the apostle. Every letter he wrote ends with pointed, practical applications of the truth he has set out.

This first letter to the Thessalonians is no exception. The closing verses of chapter 5 are wonderfully practical guidelines on how to live Christianly.

FOLLOW THE LEADER

When Paul wrote, "Respect those who work hard among you, who are over you in the Lord" (5:12), he intended that these words should govern the behavior of believers in the congregation of Thessalonica.

Unfortunately, the phrase "[those] who are over you in the Lord" seems to reflect a relationship that other Scriptures speak against. For example, Jesus said to His disciples, "You have only one Master and you are all brothers" (Matt. 23:8). Christians are to be brothers and sisters in Christ, not "over" one another. Paul's injunction to the Thessalonians, however, has to do with a different relationship. When the apostle says, "respect those who work hard among you and *stand before you* (literal Greek) *in the Lord*," he was referring to those who stood in front and led the believers when they gathered together. There is no suggestion of anyone being "over" others. What Paul was saying, therefore, was: Follow your leaders.

And he gave three guidelines that will help church members learn to follow their leaders:

1. *Respect them.* The more accurate translation would be "know them." Recognize them. Be aware of them. Do not take them for granted.

I know of churches where pastors are treated as hired servants; they are there to respond to the whims of the board of the church or the vote of the congregation. They are accorded little or no respect and at times are severely mistreated. That kind of treatment is shameful. Here the apostle is saying, "Get to know your leaders. Understand that they are people and do not ignore them."

2. *"Hold them in the highest regard"* (v. 13). In other words, value them. Understand that though your leaders may have personal idiosyncrasies that are hard to handle on occasion, their work is important; and for that reason they should be highly esteemed.

Through the centuries the church has attempted to flatter its leaders with high-sounding titles such as "bishop," "reverend," and others. But Paul is not talking about bestowing superficial names and labels. Personally, I have always appreciated the fact that during the nearly forty years I have served as pastor of Peninsula Bible Church, I have been called "Ray"—not Dr. Ray or even Brother Ray. And I'm in good company. I've noticed that in the New Testament the early church leaders, even the mighty apostles of our Lord, are all called by their first names—not Saint Peter or the Apostle John.

To "hold them in the highest regard" is not only to esteem leaders as valuable, but also to express that esteem in a practical manner. This is why Paul wrote in his first letter to Timothy, "The elders who direct the affairs of the church well are worthy of double honor" (5:17). The apostle meant that the leader should be paid twice as much salary! In other words, a double honorarium.

Recently my wife and I decided to refurbish our home. Before we knew it, some of our congregation had moved in and had begun painting, laying new floors and carpeting, working on the fences, and fixing up the yard. It was marvelous! My wife and I thought the Millennium had arrived! What a wonderful way to be held "in the highest regard in love."

3. *"Live in peace with each other"* (v. 13). This admonition suggests a deliberate refusal to create factions over individual leaders of a church. Do not group around one person at the expense of others in leadership. Do not play favorites and attack others. In 1 Timothy, Paul warns that no one may bring an accusation against an elder except on the word of two or three witnesses. Careful heed to these guidelines would prevent many a church split or fracture.

But Paul never offers advice without divine documentation, and here he reminds the Thessalonian believers of three things:

a. Leaders have been sent by the Lord. "We ask you, brothers, to respect those who work hard among you, who are over you *in the Lord*" (v. 12). Leaders are appointed by the Lord Jesus, regardless of the human process by which they are chosen. That does not mean that leaders will stay in the same position or place forever. What it means is that while they are in leadership positions, they are to be regarded as appointed by the Lord. He has sent them among us.

b. Leaders are called to "admonish you." Literally, this means "to put in mind." Leaders are to instruct and inspire you, reminding you of truth that is easily forgotten. The only voice that is speaking powerfully against the spirit of the age today—the self-centered, self-sufficient, restless spirit of the Me generation—is the voice of the church. We need to be reminded continually of the danger in that kind of philosophy. This is to be done by the leadership, who instruct, warn, and point out folly. They help us keep our feet on the right path.

c. Leaders are there to "work hard among you." Church leaders are to labor. They spend hours toiling in difficult and sometimes demeaning work. Pastors do not work only one day a week—contrary to what some people think. The ministry is a very demanding job.

A couple of years ago one of our pastors made a very interesting report to the board of elders. The report consisted of a twelve-month record of activities carried out during this man's ministry to the church. In the following section he listed the range of problems he had dealt with in his office or home over the period of a year:

> There are all forms of anger, from long-standing resentment and unforgiveness, to rebellion, violence, child-beating, mutilating, wife torture, threats against life, murder for hire, and Mafia-related revenge. There are the sexual offenses of rape, incest, sodomy, homosexuality, gang sex and swingers, bestiality, fornication, and the ever-present adultery. There are marital problems of every kind, attempted or contemplated suicide (and an occasional successful suicide), abortions, and adoptions. I see many family problems between parents, or single parents, and children. There are also the addicts of every sort—alcoholics, drugaholics, foodaholics, workaholics, sexaholics, spendaholics. There are the institutionalized, either coming from or going to a prison, hospital, detox unit, or mental facility. There is the psychotic to deal with, or the quieter legal, financial, and vocational problems, or questions about a specific passage of Scripture, or those simply wanting to know about the church.

How would you like to run into that range of problems in a twelve-month period? That is why the apostle says we are to value our leaders and to treat them with respect and love, for they work hard among us.

LIVING WITH OTHER BELIEVERS

In addressing the issue of our behavior toward others in the body of Christ, the ever-practical Paul speaks clearly and plainly, pointing out three distinct types of people: the *idle*, the *timid*, and the *weak* (v. 14).

The Idlers

"Warn those who are idle," he says. The word means literally "the disorderly," those out of step with the rest of the crowd. In Thessalonica, it meant those who had quit working because they expected the Lord to come at any moment. These people were living off the gifts of others and were not willing to work and support themselves.

"Warn them," says the apostle. Tell them to mend their ways. Do not let them go on like that. Point out to them that this kind of behavior is unacceptable.

The Timid

"Encourage the timid"; literally, the "small-souled" person, one who feels inadequate and ungifted. Paul is referring to the introverts among us—people who feel out of it, who think they do not belong and cannot contribute anything. Help these folks to find their place.

In 1 Corinthians 12, that wonderful picture of the body at work, the apostle says, "And if the ear should say, 'Because

I am not an eye, I do not belong to the body,' it would not for that reason cease to be part of the body" (12:16). There are people who feel they cannot do anything, that they have no gifts. This is wrong thinking. God has equipped all His people with gifts, and we are to help them find those gifts, give them something to do, and encourage them to do it.

The Weak Ones

"Help the weak," Paul says, targeting those whom Romans 14 describes as being "weak in the faith"—those who do not know much about the Christian life, who have not learned the truth that sets them free. Perhaps they are uncertain of their salvation, or feel guilty about the past and do not sense that they have really been forgiven by God. Whatever it may be, we are to help them, to hold them fast. That demands a little extra effort: perhaps a phone call, an invitation to lunch, or a quiet discussion about their needs. Paul is telling all of us to watch out for one another.

Paul says three special attitudes are required: (1) "be patient with everyone"; (2) "make sure that nobody pays back wrong for wrong"; and (3) "always try to be kind to each other and to everyone else" (vv. 14–15). Patience is willingness to keep trying again. Non-retaliation means that you do not try to get even with someone who may have hurt you. Helpfulness is a continual attempt to better a situation, to be part of the solution and not part of the problem.

LIVING WITH GOD

In the last section of chapter 5 we find instructions on how to behave toward God. And Paul minces no words.

1. *"Be joyful always"* (v. 16). Perhaps the better translation is "Be cheerful." Don't let things get you down.

In recent months I have had numerous phone calls from people who are at the end of themselves. The pressures under which we live today are enough to test the most stalwart among us, to rob us of peace and contentment. But a Christian has an inner resource for dealing with difficulty. James insists that we should even consider ourselves fortunate when hard times come: "Consider it pure *joy*, my brothers, whenever you face trials of many kinds" (James 1:2). Do not take it as an attack. Do not moan and groan and say, "What have I done to deserve this?" Be glad! It's good for you! Trials stretch you—make you face yourself and learn things about yourself you didn't know before. Trials lead to maturity, so "That you may be mature and complete, not lacking anything" (v. 4).

Dr. Arthur Halliday, who works with AIDS patients in our city, tells this story of his life. As a young physician, he says, he thought the world was his oyster. He was cocky and self-confident and could accomplish anything he set out to do. Then things began to fall apart. His marriage failed, and he lost his home. He had to spend hundreds of thousands of dollars with nothing to show for it. As trial after trial hit, he began to realize that life was tougher than he imagined. He found he could not handle it. After two broken marriages, he met a Christian woman who led him into a relationship with Christ, and that is when he began to grow up. What beautiful character he now displays as he labors selflessly in a ministry of compassion and help to those who are victims of AIDS. But it was the trials he went through that changed him and prepared him for this work. That is why James says that we should be joyful when trials come, because God is going to teach us something that will be of great value.

2. *Be prayerful.* Paul says, "Pray continually" (v. 17). Prayer is the method of drawing on the inner strength God provides.

My wife and I had dinner recently with the young pastor of a struggling church. He told us that one of the things that had made life difficult for him during the past year was that all the literature he read on how to be a successful pastor urged him to find a support group to reinforce his ministry. Now, I have nothing against support groups; in fact, I believe in them. God has put us in a body, and we can profit greatly from a small group of praying people around us. But this man made the mistake of thinking that success was impossible without the support of such a group, and he had been unable to find anyone else who could help and pray with him. He and his wife were very discouraged. "What shall we do?" they asked. We replied that a support group is not a necessity. God often removes all the props from our lives in order to teach us that He Himself is all we need.

Have you been there yet? Have your props been taken away and have you begun to learn that God Himself can meet your needs? If you have poured out your heart in prayer, sometimes in almost desperate prayer, you have probably already discovered that He has quiet ways of assuring you that He is El Shaddai, "the God who is enough." When you do, then you will have something to contribute to a support group. That is why Paul says, "Pray continually." When you are under pressure and in trouble, be prayerful. Lean on the inner strength God provides.

3. *Be thankful.* This seems like a hard word from Paul: "Give thanks in all circumstances, for this is God's will for you in Christ Jesus" (v. 18).

Why be thankful? Because when you are faced with a trial, you are being given an opportunity to glorify God. If you never face trials or pressures, how will anyone ever see that you have an invisible means of support, that you have a reliable source of strength that others do not know anything about? These are God-given opportunities, so be thankful *for* them and *in the process of* them.

When the early Christian leaders were arrested by the Sanhedrin, they were beaten for their faith; but they left the council rejoicing that they had been counted worthy to bear suffering for His name's sake. That is a thoroughly Christian attitude, and that is how we ought to face our trials.

Notice how the apostle underlines this truth: "This is God's will for you." The will of God is not to make some dramatic display of power or gift that is going to attract attention. It is the quiet response you make to the daily trials and circumstance in which you find yourself. Twice in this letter Paul uses the phrase, "It is God's will." First, he said, "It is God's will that you . . . avoid sexual immorality" (4:3). That is the will of God for your body! But here is the will of God for your spirit, your inner life: that you "give thanks in all circumstances." If you want to do the will of God, there are two areas in which His will is clearly set out for you: moral purity for your body, and continual thanksgiving for your spirit.

LIVING IN THE SPIRIT

How are we to react to the guidance God gives? Simple, says Paul. Do not ignore the Spirit's prompting and do not despise the Scripture's instruction (vv. 19–20).

The prompting of the Spirit always comes in two ways: First, stop doing what is wrong; and second, start doing what is right. If you are a Christian, you are familiar with the inner nudge that says, "God wants you to do something," or "God wants you to stop doing something." Paul is saying, "Give in to those feelings. When the Spirit prompts you to show love toward somebody, do it; do not hold back." I once heard of a man who said, "Sometimes when I think of how my wife works and blesses me, it's all I can do to keep from telling her how much I love her!" There is a man who was being guided by the Spirit, but quenched the Spirit. Don't do that. Go ahead and tell her you love her, even if you have to pick her up off the floor afterward!

Second, do not ignore the Scripture's wisdom. In Paul's words, "Do not treat prophecies with contempt" (v. 20). Unfortunately, because of certain cultic tendencies in our day, we think of prophesying as some special power to predict the future either for ourselves individually or for the world at large.

Dr. F. F. Bruce, one of the great expositors of our day, says prophesying is "declaring the mind of God in the power of the Spirit." In the early days of the church, before the New Testament was written, this was done orally; a prophet spoke the mind of the Spirit in an assembly. But since the writing of the Scriptures, we have very little need for any kind of prophesying other than that based upon the Bible. So for us, prophesying has become what we call expository preaching and teaching. It is opening the mind of God from the Word of God. Do not despise that, says the apostle; that is the wisdom of God telling you how to act, how to think, and how to order your life. Do not treat it lightly. Obeying its commandments will save you countless headaches and heartaches.

But, the apostle adds, "test everything" (v. 21). It is easy to imitate prophecy. Anyone can stand up and declare in a commanding voice, "This is the word of the Lord." We must learn to measure what is said against what has already been revealed. Paul commended the Bereans for their discernment, saying they were more noble than those in Thessalonica because they "received the word with all readiness of mind, and searched the scriptures daily, whether those things were so" (Acts 17:11 KJV).

Dr. Bruce tells of a saying attributed to Jesus that was often quoted by early Christian writers, though it is not found in the Gospels: "Become approved money-changers." The money-changers in the temple were occupied in changing various currencies and were constantly looking out for counterfeit coins. That is what Paul tells us to do with those who prophesy. People on every side are telling us what God wants us to do, but there is much counterfeit prophecy. Become approved money-changers. Test what is said.

Finally, Paul ends his letter with a benediction of peace: "May your whole spirit, soul and body be kept blameless at the coming of our Lord Jesus Christ . . . . He will do it" (vv. 23–24). God is able to minister to the whole person—spirit, soul, and body, and He will! Full provision has already been made—let us utilize it!

Rest on His faithfulness. Choose to obey, and He will give you power to perform; but He will not give you the power to perform until you make the choice to obey!

And persevere until the "coming of our Lord Jesus." Throughout Paul's letter this has been the great hope set before us: Jesus is coming again. God's kingdom will come on earth. There is only a limited time of testing to go through now; it cannot go on forever. I often think of the motto that used to be prominent in many homes:

> *Only one life, 'twill soon be past,*
> *Only what's done for Christ will last.*

I would like to change one word in that verse: "Only what's done *by* Christ will last." That is where the apostle leaves us: with the hope of the coming of our Lord and the resources God has provided, so that we may live in a new and different way in the midst of this modern age.

2
THESSALONIANS

THE FIRE
NEXT TIME 9
(1:1–12)

I AM GREATLY ENCOURAGED that the apostle Paul had to write a second letter to the Thessalonians to explain his first! I have had to do that on occasion. My writing is not always as clear as it could be, and I have had to attempt an explanation. The apostle's second letter was written within a few months of the first, and in it he seeks to clarify some points that were confusing the Thessalonians.

At the time of the writing of his second letter, Paul was still in the city of Corinth. The year was A.D. 50 or 51, and prior to this Timothy had been sent to Thessalonica to see how things were going in the church there. Upon his return, Timothy had reported that the Thessalonian Christians were standing steadfast against great tribulation. Paul's first letter was written in response to this report, a letter of commendation and encouragement.

But now, perhaps in a letter or a traveler's report, word had reached Paul that there was much confusion in the

Thessalonian church about the coming of the Lord. Some had apparently also protested that Paul's words of praise in the first letter were not deserved. Thus, the opening lines of the second letter, after the standard greeting, address this issue.

Paul's greeting is the same as in the first letter except that he twice repeats the words, "God our Father and the Lord Jesus Christ" (2 Thess. 1:1, 2). He is stressing the fact that the source of a Christian's strength and endurance in times of pressure is God our Father and the Lord Jesus Christ.

We, too, are living in difficult days. There is tension, war, disease, crime, unemployment, disillusionment, and every other kind of struggle. There is every reason for us also to emphasize what Paul told the Thessalonians: The Christian's resource is "God our Father and the Lord Jesus Christ." The words of a great hymn say this so well:

> *What a friend we have in Jesus,*
> *All our sins and griefs to bear.*
> *What a privilege to carry*
> *Everything to God in prayer.*

IN PRAISE OF PAIN

Under great pressure and tribulation, the church at Thessalonica was growing and thriving. For this reason Paul declares that he "ought always to thank God for you, brothers, and rightly so" (1:3). Those words of praise, for which he had been criticized in his first letter to the Thessalonians, were not based on mere courtesy or convention but on the fact of the believers' increasing spiritual vitality. Growing faith and love are marks of a healthy church, and the apostle had good reason to boast about them.

Nevertheless, something is missing. Despite their "work of faith" and their "labor of love" mentioned in the first letter, conspicuously absent is their "patience of hope" (1:3 KJV). Herein lies the problem that this letter was written to correct. Paul has learned that the Thessalonian Christians are still confused and uncertain about the coming of the Lord. They are not sure what they are waiting for.

And Paul knows that without hope, the work of faith and the labor of love will be undermined. History bears out the fact that when hope is lost in the face of persecution, faith and love are soon lost as well.

We do not know exactly how these young Christians suffered. Some had probably been arrested, thrown in jail, and beaten. Perhaps their homes had been confiscated and heavy fines levied against them, or perhaps the privileges of citizenship had been denied them. In all likelihood they were undergoing the same trials as Christians today who are living under Communist dictatorships. But whatever form this persecution took, the apostle says—and do not miss this— their endurance in the face of tremendous pressure was evidence that God was at work among them!

It is impossible to endure, to hang in there, Paul says, unless you are being strengthened by the Spirit of God. People today who are caught up in the cross fire of adversity and outright attack give up very easily unless there is some inner resource to provide strength.

But the Thessalonians were enduring; and Paul declares that, in at least three ways, this was proof positive of God at work among them.

1. *Suffering is used to prepare us for the kingdom reign with God.* God was making the Thessalonian Christians "worthy of the kingdom of God" (v. 5). Actually this phrase should be rendered, "revealing that you are worthy." By their en-

durance in suffering God was showing the Thessalonians that they were worthy of the kingdom of God because of their faith in Christ. The fact that they could stand up under pressure was evidence that they had been truly removed from Satan's kingdom of darkness and placed in the kingdom of the Son of God's love. What a great word this is, especially for young people today! Holding out against the pressures of drug traffic, sexual promiscuity, and other lures of the world is proof that God is at work in your life.

2. *Suffering is used to reveal God's condemnation of the world.* He is going to "pay back trouble to those who trouble you" (v. 6). Hebrews 11 is the record of the great heroes of our faith: Abraham, Isaac, Moses, Sarah, and other Old Testament worthies. But there is another group whose names are not listed. These "faced jeers and flogging, while still others were chained and put in prison. They were stoned; they were sawed in two; they were put to death by the sword. They went about in sheepskins and goatskins, destitute, persecuted and mistreated—*the world was not worthy of them*" (vv. 36–38).

God's value standard is quite different from that of society. You may not be anyone in the eyes of the world, but if you are standing fast in your Christian faith in the face of trials and struggles, you are someone in the eyes of God. And someday, all this shall be revealed.

Thus Paul assures the Thessalonians that God is going to even the score: "God is just; He will pay back trouble to those who trouble you and give relief to you who are troubled, and to us as well." That word *relief* in the Greek is *anesin*. What do you do when you have a headache? You take an Anacin and you get relief! In His own timing, when Jesus comes, He will bring relief, visible on a world-wide scale.

On a trip to Israel we visited the great Holocaust memorial in Jerusalem. There, the terrible tortures to which the Jews were subjected—the Nazi death camps, the gas chambers of Buchenwald and Auschwitz and others—are well remembered. The newspaper reports, the fearsome scenes that the Allies found when they liberated these camps, and other memorabilia are on display, mute testimony that these atrocities will forever live in human memory.

Even more touching is the new memorial that has been built in honor of the children of the Holocaust. Visiting this memorial was one of the most moving experiences of my life. The hall is almost totally dark, illuminated by only a few candles, but hundreds of mirrors reflect the light so the impression is that of thousands of candles burning. There in the gloom I felt as though I were standing at the judgment bar of God! Hidden voices endlessly call out the names of children who were tortured and murdered by the Nazis. It is Israel's way of saying that these children will never be forgotten. Not one injustice, not one humiliation, not one act of pain or torture will ever be forgotten. God is telling us the same thing in Paul's second letter to the Thessalonians. He will bring affliction to those who afflict, and rest and relief to those who are afflicted.

THE JUDGMENT OF FLAMING FIRE

How long will it be? How long before those who have suffered will be vindicated? Paul tells us: "When the Lord Jesus is revealed from heaven in blazing fire with his powerful angels" (vv. 7–8).

This event is the climax of the whole series of events that Scripture calls the *parousia*, the presence of Jesus. After the

Tribulation, He will manifest Himself, "unveil" Himself in open glory—"in blazing fire," accompanied by His powerful angels—to judge the world and begin His earthly reign of a thousand years.

This agrees exactly with our Lord's own words uttered on the Mount of Olives shortly before His crucifixion, as reported by Matthew: "Immediately after the distress of those days . . . all the nations of the earth will mourn. They will see the Son of Man coming on the clouds of the sky, with power and great glory" (Matt. 24:29–30).

Here the apostle is describing two events that will take place at that time: first, the judgment of the rebels of earth; and second, the presentation in glory of the true believers in the Lord—the same event described in Matthew 25 as the Great Judgment of the sheep and the goats. Judgment will fall upon two classes of people: "those who do not know God" and those who "do not obey the gospel of our Lord Jesus" (2 Thess. 1:8).

Those Who Lack Knowledge

I suppose there is no question asked of Bible teachers more frequently than "What happens to those who never hear the gospel?" The simple answer is that they will suffer the vengeance of the Lord.

Many of you are asking, why? If they have never heard the gospel, how can God justly judge them? The answer is: Because they have rejected the revelation of God in nature. No one lives in total ignorance of God. He is revealing Himself all the time, both in our own human nature and in the world of nature about us. This is clearly described in Paul's letter to the Romans, where he says, "men are without excuse" (Rom. 1:19–20).

We have great difficulty with that concept. There is something in all of us that rejects the thought of punishment. Like children, we do not enjoy having to face the consequences of our own choices. But that is what Paul is talking about here. God has revealed Himself clearly to all His creatures. He is the Creator. He is in charge of the world. Every single force at work in the universe comes from His hand and is under His control. Anyone who thinks about the strange and wonderful workings of his or her own body is aware that only a vastly superior Being could have engineered such a magnificent machine.

Yet the whole thrust of society today is to eliminate God from His creation, to give no recognition to the fact that He is behind all things. Certainly there is no attempt to be thankful to Him. That is why Paul levels this charge against the whole human race. For it is not merely primitive savages who fail to acknowledge God or be thankful to Him. People all over this sophisticated country and throughout our so-called civilized world are just as guilty.

Nor does Paul mean that a mere recognition of God guarantees automatic redemption. It still remains true that no one can come to the Father except through Jesus. Our Lord Himself said so. But what it does mean is that God Himself will make sure that those who recognize His revelation in nature and begin to seek Him will have an opportunity to hear about Jesus. For this reason missionaries have been sent to every corner of the globe.

The Arrogant Rebels

Then there are those who have heard the gospel but have rejected it and thereby turned their backs on the offer of grace. Millions of rebels roam the earth, and thousands of them sit in churches in our own land. They have heard the good news that if they surrender their lives to Jesus, if they recognize that they are not their own but have been bought with a price, they will be redeemed; they will be changed; they will be saved. They have heard, but they have turned their backs and walked away time and time again.

What happens to them? How plainly the apostle puts it: "They will be punished with everlasting destruction and shut out from the presence of the Lord and from the majesty of his power" (v. 9).

Exclusion! Banishment! Separation! But not annihilation! Some interpret these verses to mean that when people die, their existence also ends; that they go out like the snuffed light of a candle and are no more. But Scripture never describes death in those terms; rather, it speaks of "everlasting destruction." The word here is "ruin," the loss of everything that makes life worthwhile.

Some folks like to make jokes about hell, but if you will simply read the Scriptures, you will soon find that hell is no joking matter. Jesus Himself speaks of hell more often than anyone else in the New Testament. Others flippantly remark that they wouldn't mind going to hell since "all their friends are going to be there." They speak of hell as if it were one great "Animal House," with a fraternity party going on forever, where you can waste yourself with no one to stop you. That is definitely not the picture painted in Scripture.

C. S. Lewis wrote: "In hell, everybody will be at an infinite distance from everybody else." What a vision of loneliness and emptiness! The apostle Jude describes those in hell as "wandering stars, for whom blackest darkness has been reserved forever" (Jude 13). Sobering words indeed!

The following excerpt is taken from a sermon preached on this subject by Bill Hybels, a young Chicago pastor who each Sunday morning addresses some ten thousand people, many of whom are unsaved. Of hell, he says:

> One writer calls it the bottomless pit. And that conjures up dreamlike feelings of falling away—falling, falling, falling. You've all had dreams like that, where when you woke your heart was beating because you were falling. Picture in your mind hanging over a precipice, and God is hanging onto you, and you're hanging onto him. And you decide you don't need him anymore. So you let go. But the moment you let go you know you made a mistake. You're falling and every moment you fall farther and farther away from the only source of help and truth and love, and you realize you made a mistake and you can't get back up and you fall farther and faster and farther and faster into spiritual oblivion, and you know you're going the wrong direction and you'd give anything to go back but you can't and you fall and you fall and you fall and you fall. How long? Forever. And all the while you're falling you're saying, "I'm farther now, I'm farther. I'm farther from the only source of hope, truth, and love." In hell there is never the bliss of annihilation. You'd give anything for annihilation, but it's unavailable, only the conscious continuation of emotional anguish, physical anguish, relational anguish, and spiritual anguish forever.

What terrible sin must be committed to merit such an end? Turning one's back on God's offer of grace, the Scriptures tell us. God does not want anyone to perish like that, of course. He says so. And He has gone through terrible agony to keep it from happening. But no matter how much we dislike passages like this, two truths always emerge.

First, this sentence is nothing more than justice being carried out. It is not meanness, not cruelty, not capriciousness, but justice on God's part. It is His righteous reaction to cosmic treason on man's part. That is what turning your back on Jesus means: treason against the King of the universe.

And secondly, the sentence is self-imposed. It is what those involved have always wanted: freedom from God. Everything in their life has said, "I don't want God messing up my plans and telling me what to do." There comes a time when you either say to God, "Thy will be done," or else God says to you, "Thy will be done." What you want is what you eventually get!

REFLECTION OF GLORY

Fortunately, the story does not end with those sad words. There is a marvelous ending for "all those who have believed." Notice the little word *all*. The verse continues: "This includes you, because you believed our testimony" (v. 10).

God will not glorify us because we have lived a good, decent life nor because we have earned a qualifying number of spiritual merit badges. Rather, our glorification is based upon the fact that we have believed that Another did something for us. Another died in our place, and God has honored the death of that Other to such a degree that He offers to accept us, with our terrible record of failure and defeat, and to offer us an eternity of delight and glory with Him.

Paul describes the glory of Jesus that will be seen "in his holy people," and the way these believers cause people to marvel at what God has done in human lives. It is not Jesus Himself and His glory that is described, but the saints *reflecting* the glory of Jesus. The whole universe will marvel!

The apostle John says in his first letter: "What we will be has not yet been made known. But we know that when he appears, we shall be like him, for we shall see him as he is" (1 John 3:2). That is what Paul calls in Romans 8:19, "the day of the manifestation of the sons of God" (KJV)—when the curtain is lifted and the world will see at last what God has been doing with His people through all these ages, how He has been changing them on the inside.

As a young Christian, I remember singing:

Holy, holy, holy, is what the angels sing,
And I expect to help them make the courts of heaven ring.
But when we sing redemption's story,
They must fold their wings,
For angels never felt the joy that our salvation brings.

There is a glory, a joy, known only by the redeemed. That marvelous manifestation of the grace and glory of God will be evident in those who have been changed by His grace.

Finally, Paul prays for the Thessalonians—and for us. He is saying: "Hold on. Keep steady. Remain faithful. You have the *resolve* to do so in the desire given you by the Spirit; you have the *faith* to do so in the basis of fact revealed in the Scripture, and you have the *power* to do so since God Himself dwells in you." All this, "according to the grace of our God and the Lord Jesus Christ." Granted that it may sometimes be hard. It is not easy to stand for Christ in your family when perhaps some members are against you. It is not easy to be loving, winsome, and warm toward those who are cruel and caustic to you at work. This can be a tough, brutal, ruthless world; Scripture faces those facts head on. But we are constantly reminded that the Lord Jesus is even now being glorified when we hold steady, when we do not give up, when we do not allow ourselves to fall into evil practices, but are able to say no and walk away from them. That is when Jesus is being glorified, says the apostle.

And, says Paul, you also are being glorified. Inner changes are taking place in your life that you cannot see. Others may be able to catch a glimpse of them now and then. But when the Lord Jesus shows us off before the whole world at the time of the unveiling of His presence, the glory He has been shaping within us will blaze forth to such a degree that the whole universe will gasp!

What a hope! What motivation to keep on keeping on!

THE MAN WHO CLAIMS TO BE GOD

10

(2:1–12)

ONE OF THE QUESTIONS that has been a battleground through the decades is: Will the church still be here on earth during the Tribulation? Will the Lord come for His church before the great time of trouble; will He come in the middle of it; or will the church, in fact, go through the Tribulation, with Jesus coming at the end?

This is a much-debated and controversial issue. Certain of the Scriptures covering this matter are difficult to understand, leading to differences of opinion among believers.

For almost fifty years I have studied the passage in 2 Thessalonians 2:1–12, have read all the arguments pro and con, have considered the three evangelical positions on Jesus' second coming—a pre, mid, or post-tribulational coming—and I would like to point out why I believe the Scriptures teach that the church will not go through the great Tribulation, and why I reject the arguments of the post-tribulationalists.

Typical of Paul's letters is his clear statement of purpose: To relate the coming, the *parousia*, of the Lord Jesus to our assembling to meet Him, (or what is commonly known as the rapture of the church) described in 1 Thessalonians 4:16–17. If we think of the coming of the Lord as but a single event occurring within a twenty-four-hour period, we will conclude that this "assembling ourselves to meet him" is part of that event; and thus that the Lord's appearing in glory does not come until the end of the Tribulation, with the Rapture a part of it.

But when we remember that the word *parousia* means "presence" (though it is frequently translated "coming"), it suggests a series of events, during which Jesus is present for the whole time. If this is our viewpoint, then what Paul is proposing to discuss is: At what point does our assembling to meet Jesus come in that series of events? In other words: When does the Rapture take place?[1]

THE TERRIBLE DAY OF THE LORD

According to Paul, the Thessalonian believers were deeply agitated and disturbed. Something or someone had obviously promoted the idea that the terrible Day of the Lord had already begun and that they were even now experiencing it.

---

[1]For a more complete explanation see Appendix.

In his first letter to them, Paul described that day as one of sudden destruction, with no escape possible, as with a woman in labor (1 Thess. 5:3). The Old Testament prophets had described it as a day of distress and anguish, ruin and devastation.

Under the Roman authorities, the Thessalonians were no doubt going through a time of great persecution. Perhaps someone in their assembly had uttered a prophecy or had interpreted a passage of Scripture to the effect that the Day of the Lord had already come. Perhaps, as Paul himself suggested, a letter purportedly written by him was read, saying that the day of the Lord's wrath had arrived.

Regardless of the reason, the result was not, as the RSV text suggests, that they were "excited" at the prospect of Jesus' soon coming. If the passage is read that way, it does appear that the church will go through the Tribulation. If the Lord was not coming until the end of that time of trouble and it had already begun, then they could now become excited in "wild anticipation of the immediate return of Christ," as one commentator puts it.

But this is not the meaning of those words! The phrase literally reads, "You were shaken out of your minds" or, to put it in the vernacular, "all shook up." Linked with this is a word that can only be translated "disturbed." (The same word is translated "alarmed" in Mark 13:7 RSV.) They were not excited about the coming of the Lord. Rather, they were scared out of their minds! It was sweaty palms and white knuckles all the way!

Back in the thirties when I was a young Christian, I read a novel popular among believers at the time, entitled *In the Twinkling of an Eye*. It was the story of several members of a family who returned home one day to find that the table was set and everything ready for dinner, but no one was there.

Upon investigation, they discovered that the rest of the family and some of their friends had disappeared. Then it dawned on them that the Rapture had occurred. The true church had been taken up, and they had been left behind. They were church members and knew enough about the Bible to know that they were headed for a terrible time of trouble. They were scared out of their wits!

I know the feeling also. Once I entered a room where I expected to find a group of Christians. The room was strewn with papers. Books were lying open on tables. But not one person was to be seen. I thought to myself, "Oh! I've missed it!"

Now why would a pretribulational Christian think so negatively? Because at such times there is enough self-doubt in all of us that we wonder about the authenticity of our experience. When our Lord said to the disciples in the Upper Room, "One of you will betray me," every one of them responded, "Surely not I, Lord?" Their questions betrayed their doubt about the validity of their own faith.

It was this condition the apostle was describing. The Thessalonians thought the Rapture had occurred and they had somehow missed it, and now the Day of the Lord had arrived.

RETHINKING THE RAPTURE

Notice that Paul does *not* say to the distressed Thessalonian believers: "Now don't worry. If the Day of the Lord had come, you would not be here; you would have been raptured." The fact that Paul does not say this is cited by the post-tribulationalists, who argue that Paul taught a post-tribulational coming.

We must ask ourselves why he did not say that. The answer is likely that Paul was not sure that all of the Thessalonians who claimed to be believers were truly Christians. Consequently he was very careful not to risk giving them a false sense of assurance by saying glibly: "If you believe in Christ, then you are safe."

Many lost people believe themselves to be Christians. They have gone along with the outward appearances of Christianity, but they have never surrendered their inner wills to the Lord. If Paul had told such nominal Christians in Thessalonica that they would certainly be raptured, he would have sealed them into a false view of their security.

As a matter of fact, he does tell them that Christians will be raptured before the Tribulation, but he does so in a guarded and subtle way.

I must also point out that there is considerable evidence that the word translated "rebellion" or "apostasy" should more properly be translated "the departure." Read that way, the apostle is clearly saying that the Day of the Lord cannot come until the departure (of the church) has first taken place. (For further information, see *Rethinking the Rapture* by Dr. E. Schuyler English.)

For the sake of argument, however, let's accept the translation as "apostasy" or "rebellion." What Paul is saying, then, is that the unmistakable sign that the Day of the Lord has begun is that the Man of Lawlessness will have been revealed.

THE HOPELESSLY LOST ONE

Jesus Himself speaks of this historical personage in the Olivet discourse of Matthew 24: "So when you see standing in the holy place '*the abomination that causes desolation,*' spoken of through the prophet Daniel . . . then, there will be great distress, unequaled from the beginning of the world until now—and never to be equaled again" (vv. 15, 21).

This person—announced first by the prophet Daniel, then by Jesus, and presented by Paul—is the long-expected Antichrist, the false Messiah, the "hopelessly lost one," the "son of perdition." Only one other person in the New Testament is called by that name: Judas, the betrayer of our Lord. Jesus refers to the Antichrist as "standing in the holy place . . . 'the abomination that causes desolation'" (Matt. 24:15).

Paul describes him as one who "will oppose and will exalt himself over everything that is called God or is worshiped, so that he sets himself up in God's temple, proclaiming himself to be God" (2 Thess. 2:4), which is exactly what Jesus was saying. This man will take his place in the temple as an "abomination that causes desolation."

Paul reminds the Thessalonians that he told them about this when he was with them (v. 5). The reference here, therefore, is but a footnote to that previous teaching.

THE RESTRAINER

According to the apostle, the Day of the Lord cannot come until the Man of Lawlessness is revealed. But the Man of Lawlessness cannot be revealed, Paul says, until some restraining power is taken out of the way (v. 6). What is that restraining power? The apostle's answer is short and to the point: "You know what it is." There was no need to tell the Thessalonians; they already knew!

It is interesting that the word the apostle employs here for "know" is not the word *ginosko*, which means "to learn by experience." Rather, it is the word *oido*, which means "to know by insight, by inner information." I believe that every born-again Christian knows "by inner information" what it is that restrains evil. I have often asked young Christians: "Since Christ has come into your life have you found anything that restrains evil in you?" Invariably the answer is: "Oh, yes, *everything* is different. I no longer have the same desires now that the Lord has come into my life." The Holy Spirit has come in; thus, God Himself dwells within the believer, restraining the evil he would otherwise do.

In his letter to the Galatians, Paul teaches that the desires of our flesh are opposed by the desires of the Spirit, and the Spirit's desires are opposed by the flesh, "so that you do not do what you want" (Gal. 5:17). A mighty power is at work restraining evil in believers and, through believers, restraining evil in the world. That is why Jesus said, "You [believers] are the salt of the earth," preserving this world from decay and corruption. Believers are also the light of the world, for while they are in the world, they relieve the terrible darkness around by means of the Holy Spirit.

What is it about humanity that makes it so difficult for us to correct the conditions that are destroying us? Why is drug trafficking so impossible to stop when the terrible results are clearly evident? Why do alcoholics return again and again to their habit even when they can see that alcoholism wrecks homes, families, and even their own lives? Why are we still wrestling with the same problems that people wrestled with five thousand years before Christ? Paul calls it a mystery: "the mystery of lawlessness"—the secret of universal evil (2 Thess. 2:7 RSV).

But there is also a positive note to this restraint. Today a number of Jews in Jerusalem, Jews with powerful political connections, have committed themselves—including their lives and possessions—to rebuilding the temple. For several years their efforts have been totally frustrated; they are not making any progress. Why? Because something or Someone is restraining them!

A temple will one day be built on the spot where the Dome of the Rock now stands, and that is the place where the Man of Lawlessness will take his seat and proclaim himself to be God. Why the delay? Because the time has not yet come. The Restrainer is still at work. Just as God would not destroy the earth until Noah and his family had entered the ark (a picture of being "with Christ"), and just as God would not rain judgment on the cities of Sodom and Gomorrah until Lot and his family had first been removed, so God will not begin the last terrible judgment upon this earth until the church has been removed. The Spirit-indwelt church is the restraining force!

In the sixties and seventies our society experienced a terrible incursion of evil with a breakdown of morals on every side and the rise of previously unacceptable public practices. This happened because the church had failed to live as God had called it to live. Christians had begun to live for themselves instead of for the Lord. What tremendous power Christians could wield in the world today if only they knew who they are called to be. And what tremendous evil they permit in the world when they refuse to live as God wants them to live.

How long does the Restrainer operate? Paul gives us a clue: "The one who now holds it back will continue to do so *til* he is taken out of the way" (v. 7). When translated literally, that phrase "out of the way" is "out of the midst." We are reminded of Paul's word about the church: "We will not all sleep, but we will all be changed—in a flash, in the twinkling of an eye" (1 Cor. 15:51–52). The Spirit-indwelt church will be removed suddenly, "out of the midst" of the world.

Then, says Paul, "the lawless one will be revealed, whom the Lord Jesus will overthrow with the breath of his mouth and destroy by the splendor of his coming" (v. 8). When the church, the Spirit's restraining instrument, is removed, then the work of the Lawless One begins. From Revelation and from Daniel we learn that this work will last for three and a half years, but it will end with "his appearing and his coming"—literally, "the unveiling of the presence of Jesus." Jesus, with His church, has been here all through the Tribulation working behind the scenes, but now He will be made visible; and it is that unveiling that will destroy the Antichrist. Our Lord will utter a word and the Man of Lawlessness will be destroyed (Rev. 20:10).

THE SEDUCTION OF CHRISTIANITY

In verses 9 through 12, Paul cites the methods used by the Man of Lawlessness to spread evil throughout the world. While you may feel these verses do not apply to born-again believers who will be safely removed before the end, remember Paul's warning that the "mystery of lawlessness is *already* at work" (v. 7 RSV).

First, *its origin is Satan, already at work behind the scenes.* "Our struggle is not against flesh and blood, but against the rulers, against the authorities, against the powers of this dark world" (Eph. 6:12).

Second, *Satan gains a following with counterfeit miracles.* In recent days we have seen a revival of interest in healing miracles. Some of them are real, but many of them are counterfeit. These healings claim to showcase God's hand at work, but they are either psychological in nature or demonically inspired. Great care needs to be exercised in this area.

Third, *Satan employs various forms of deceptive evil:* Many life-styles or substances that promise fulfillment are ultimately destructive. Drugs, alcohol, perverted forms of sexuality, gambling, and adulterous affairs may appear rewarding, but the end result is always pain, heartache, and loss.

Fourth, *this approach makes its appeal to those who refuse "to love the truth,"* who have no time for the Scriptures, who refuse to judge themselves and will not listen to anyone who lovingly tries to point out that what they are doing is wrong. Such people have set their feet upon a downward path.

Fifth, *this mindset opens the door for the ultimate delusion:* belief in what the Scriptures call "the lie." That lie is: "You can be God in your own world. Really! You can run your own life. You can do whatever you want." The lie was spawned in the Garden of Eden, and it has tainted the world ever since. People who have been deceived into believing that "the lie" is "the life" are following blindly. That, says the apostle, will become a worldwide condition under the influence of this evil person called the Man of Lawlessness. It is humanism, the worship of man, in its ultimate form.

DAY OF GRACE

If it is true, as the apostle seems to be underscoring in this passage, that the Day of the Lord has not yet come, then today is still the day of grace! Unbelievers can still open their eyes and believe the truth. The unrighteous can turn to Jesus and be redeemed and belong to that crowd who, not because of their own righteousness but because they have trusted the righteousness of Another, will be caught up with the Lord before the great day of trouble begins on earth.

Where do you stand? Have you surrendered your life to Christ? Do you belong to Him? Does He run your affairs? Do you listen to His words? Do you love Him and follow Him? If not, this is a moment when you can make that decision. You can say: "Lord Jesus, I invite You to enter my life, to take it over. Help me to follow You and walk in the way of righteousness."

Jesus says: "Here I am! I stand at the door and knock. If anyone hears my voice and opens the door, I will come in and eat with him" (Rev. 3:20). This is His promise. Open that door to Him.

STAND FIRM | *11*

(2:13—3:5)

*A*S A BOY GROWING UP in Montana, I loved to read stories of the wild West. These tales convinced me that those days were perilous times when hostile Indian bands roamed about, seeking victims to torture and scalp; when lawless gunmen waited in saloons, ready to shoot down anyone who crossed them; and when entire towns could be wiped out overnight by terrible plagues. In the nineteenth century, it seemed to me, life was cheap and fraught with great danger.

But times of peril have apparently come upon us again. Today innocent tourists are kidnapped and held hostage for months and even years. Seemingly safe office buildings are invaded by ruthless killers who leave a trail of death and destruction in their wake. Our public transportation system is barraged by stone-throwing mobs. A fearsome AIDS epidemic threatens to decimate our population. People lock themselves into their homes and live in fear and terror. Children murder their parents over trivial issues. And in the midst of all this, a lusty, bawdy, godless life-style gains more followers every day.

Faced with these conditions, many are saying it is difficult to maintain faith in a God of love, power, and justice. To them it seems preferable to compromise with the world rather than challenge it. Compromise has become the spirit of the age. Because of this, our hearts easily despair, and discouragement seeps into our souls.

Things have not changed much in two thousand years, so Paul's letters of encouragement to the Thessalonians are just as relevant for us today as they were then.

Following Paul's description of the terrible conditions that will befall the world under the Antichrist at the end of the age comes a wonderful passage of comfort and assurance, signaled by that pivotal word *but:* "But we ought always to thank God for you, brothers loved by the Lord, because from the beginning God chose you to be saved through the sanctifying work of the Spirit and through belief in the truth. He called you to this through our gospel, that you might share in the glory of our Lord Jesus Christ. So then, brothers, stand firm and hold to the teachings we passed on to you, whether by word of mouth or by letter" (vv. 13–15).

No matter how bad things become, the apostle says, Christians are expected to be different! And he tells us what makes that difference possible in this marvelous passage packed with profound truth.

If I could confer a degree on the apostle Paul, I would endow him with the "M.T.T." degree, which would stand for Master of Thumbnail Theology! In these highly condensed verses are found seven aspects of truth that the Thessalonians greatly needed to steady them through those dangerous days:

WHY CHRISTIANS ARE DIFFERENT

1. *The process of standing firm in the midst of a troubled world begins with the love of God for mankind.* "We ought always to thank God for you, brothers *loved by the Lord.*" We seem to resist believing this truth despite the fact that the Bible lays much emphasis on God's love for us. Although we hide from others the mess we have made of our lives, we are conscious of our own failures; we know we have not even measured up to our own hopes and dreams, let alone God's expectations for us. Thus we have a hard time believing that God could love us. But Scripture everywhere asserts this. Perhaps the most often quoted verse in the New Testament says it best: "God so loved the world that he gave his one and only Son, that whoever believes in him shall not perish but have eternal life" (John 3:16). How amazing to know that God loves us even though He knows everything about us! He knows our likes and dislikes, the wrong things we have done, the evil thoughts, the whole sorry mess—yet He still loves us. I am reminded of the jingle that expresses this so well:

> *Isn't it odd, that a Being*
> *like God,*
> *Who sees the facade,*
> *still loves the clod*
> *He made out of sod;*
> *now isn't that odd?*

What a wondrous thing it is to know that God loves our broken and hurting race!

2. *Because God loves us, He chose us.* He calls us individually, drawing us to Himself. No one knows why God chooses one and not another. That is a great mystery, which

exercises the minds of theologians and, indeed, just about everyone who reads the Bible, for Scripture gives us little help in this matter. But do not make the mistake of thinking that God looked down through the centuries and when He foresaw those who would believe the gospel, He wrote their names in the Book of Life. Scripture tells us otherwise. If you are struggling with this truth, you are not alone. Jesus put it plainly, however, when He said, "No one can come to me unless the Father who sent me draws him!" (John 6:44). More than any other verse in Scripture perhaps, those words express the fact of God's call.

3. *The purpose God has in mind in calling us is that we might be saved.* His objective is salvation. That word gathers up a great deal of truth in Scripture. It includes conversion and regeneration, the indwelling of the Holy Spirit, and other changes that occur. Fundamentally, salvation means that our relationship to God has been altered. He no longer looks upon us as aliens and strangers, drifting along with a wicked and fallen world; rather, He views us as children, dear ones, who have become His through faith in His Son. Through the process of salvation we have been selected out of the perishing world around us and destined for glory.

4. *The process is "through the sanctifying work of the Spirit."* That is God's part. Theologians debate whether this last word should be translated with a capital S: *Spirit*, referring to the Holy Spirit, or a small s, referring to the human *spirit*. But it does not make any difference; for when you come to Christ your human spirit is invaded by the Holy Spirit. This is what the Bible calls "regeneration," being born again, a new beginning. What a change that makes in a man or woman, boy or girl!

I recently read the story of a boy who loved to get into fights and scrapes to show how tough he was. When he went to a church meeting at sixteen, however, the Spirit of God touched him and he came to Christ. Almost immediately he knew he was forever changed. He no longer wanted to fight but to help people. That fundamental change in his disposition was a sign of his regeneration, by means of the invasion of the Holy Spirit.

5. *The human side of that same process is belief "in the truth."* I do not think it is possible to say which comes first: whether you believe in the truth before you are invaded by the Spirit, or whether you are invaded by the Spirit and then you believe the truth. But somewhere along the line a choice of the will must be made. You cannot come to Christ by merely sitting in church. You must believe that what God has said applies to you; that what He says He will do He is prepared to do.

6. *The step that brings us to belief is to be called through the gospel.* Here Paul is referring to the teaching and proclamation of the good news. Before we can believe, we must hear what God offers to do. Perhaps it was in a conversation somewhere, or through reading the Bible, or after hearing something said in church, in an evangelistic meeting, or on television. You heard what God promised to do for Christ's sake, and you believed what you heard. Thus you were changed by the Spirit.

7. *God's goal is "that you might share in the glory of our Lord Jesus Christ."* What a fabulous promise! That we should someday share the triumph of the Cross with Jesus Himself is the staggering assurance of Scripture. No matter how obscure and unknown we may have been on earth, God will one day unveil before the whole universe what He has been doing through the centuries in bringing together a people who will share His glory.

To the Colossians, Paul said, "When Christ, who is your life, appears, then you also will appear with him" (Col. 3:4). The writer of Hebrews says that God is "bringing many sons to glory" (Heb. 2:10). That is God's work throughout history and in our world today.

The late Dr. Donald Grey Barnhouse, well-known Bible expositor and one of America's outstanding preachers, had a gift for stating truth briefly and concisely. He said:

> *We have a relationship that can never be changed:*
> *we are children of the Most High.*
> *We have a righteousness that can never be tarnished:*
> *the very righteousness of Christ Himself.*
> *We have a resource that can never be diminished:*
> *the power of the Spirit of God.*
> *We have a peace that can never be destroyed:*
> *it is the God of Peace Himself.*
> *We have a joy that can never be surpassed:*
> *the Scriptures call it "joy unspeakable and full of glory."*
> *We have a love that will never let us go:*
> *God's unconditional love.*
> *We have an Intercessor whose prayers can never go unanswered:*
> *the Spirit of Christ within us.*
> *We have a Sovereign Lord who can never lose control:*
> *the King of Kings Himself.*

If all that is true, then it is no wonder that the apostle goes on to say to the Thessalonians: "So then, brothers . . . ." Paul was saying: "As a result of all this, brothers, stand firm and hold to the teachings we passed on to you, whether by word of mouth or by letter" (2 Thess. 2:15). Two activities were possible, despite the hard times they were going through. They could "stand firm," and they could "hold to the teachings." Stand firm: "Do not give in under pressure." Hold to the teachings: "Do not give up the truth."

Stand Firm

We already have what it takes to stand firm, Paul said. What we need to do is to draw upon the resources God has made available and choose to live accordingly. Take God at His word! How sorely our generation of Christians needs to hear these words. There is no reason to quit or to give in to evil. When I hear Christians say, "I couldn't help myself," I know they are deceiving themselves. Christians *can* help themselves; that is why God gives them the Holy Spirit.

A man who was formerly a pastor in this area told a friend that he had to quit the pastorate because "the pressure became too great." Again, that is self-deception. The promise of Scripture is: "God is faithful; he will not let you be tempted beyond what you can bear. But when you are tempted, he will also provide a way out so that you can stand up under it" (1 Cor. 10:13). Thousands can testify that these words are true. God has given us what it takes to handle pressure. What we need to do is to review our resources.

I once heard the story of an old Navajo Indian in Arizona who became a very wealthy man when oil was discovered on his land. But wealth did not change him. He went on living just as he had before while the money piled up in the bank. Every now and then, however, the old man would visit the bank and say to the banker, "Crops all dried up; sheep all dead; cattle all stolen." The banker knew exactly what to do. He would take the old man into the vault, seat him at a table, and place several bags of silver dollars in front of him for him to count. After a while the man would come out and say, "Crops fine; sheep all alive; cattle all back." Why the change? He had simply reviewed his resources and reminded himself of what he had to fall back on. This is what believers must do when the pressure comes. When we feel like complaining and murmuring, let us remember who we are in Him and what He has promised us for times of stress.

A young pastor called me recently. He was in despair. A crisis had erupted in his church and everything seemed to be falling apart. His ministry of preaching the truth in great power had come under the attack of the enemy, and he was ready to give up. I steadied him by taking him back, step by step, over what God had made him to be, what his resources were, and what and Whom he could count on. I reminded him of the Israelites at the edge of the Red Sea. God did not say to them, "Go out into the water and drown." He told them, "I will see you through to the other side." That is what God is saying to us too: Stand firm!

Hold to the Teachings

When Paul told the Thessalonians, "Hold to the teachings we passed on to you, whether by word of mouth or by letter," he was speaking of apostolic truth (2:15). Our New Testament comes to us from the hands of apostles who heard the Lord Jesus, having been taught directly by Him while He was still on earth or later through appearances or visions. The KJV and the RSV call these teachings "traditions," but they are not the traditions of men. This is no "Fiddler on the Roof," endlessly playing over the customs of the past! These are revelations of reality from the mind of God, who sees things absolutely the way they are. These are truths that were verbally imparted to people of the first century by the apostles, and which have come down to us by means of letters from their hands.

In 1 Corinthians 11:2 (RSV) the apostle commends the Corinthians because they "maintain the traditions" he had delivered to them. One of those was the Lord's Table, God's visual aid to help us grasp the mystery and marvel of the death and resurrection of our Lord, what it cost Him, and what it means to us now in terms of new life and resurrection power. As we gather at the Lord's Table, we "maintain the traditions."

When we read and study the Word, we maintain the apostolic traditions delivered to men and women. It is impossible to *stand firm* unless we also *hold to* the traditions. A church that begins to forsake apostolic truth soon falls into error and weakness. More than once we have been confronted with the tragic news of a nationally known television evangelist who has ruined his life through sexual misconduct. The world will leap on this, claiming that Christians are no different from non-Christians. But God expects His people to stand firm because they hold to the traditions of the truth. Weakness quickly follows when any individual or church forsakes the apostolic teaching.

Unfortunately, the churches of our land are filled with biblical illiterates. Not only do many think that an epistle is the wife of an apostle, and that Sodom and Gomorrah were lovers, but even worse, they do not understand the doctrine of justification by faith, or the difference between the spirit and the flesh, or what the New Covenant means. Because they do not know these things, they are living continually under the domain of the Evil One and doing his will even though they are believers in Christ. Jesus said to the Pharisees: "You diligently study the Scriptures because you think that by them you possess eternal life. These are the

Scriptures that testify about me" (John 5:39)! Do not look into the Scriptures to find rules for how to live, but search them to find Christ, the Refuge and Resource of the believer at all times.

THE POWER TO HOLD ON

When you are in trouble, expect God, who is your defense, to supply strength so that you can hold steady. Watch Him as He unfolds a solution to your difficulty.

The Thessalonians had already experienced this supply when they first came to Christ: He "who loved us and by his grace gave us eternal encouragement" (a sense of acceptance before Him), said Paul, also gave us "good hope" (the promise of a different destiny). All of that is already ours "by his grace"— God's free gift to us. Paul fully expected that state to continue: God will "encourage your hearts" (reassure you) and "strengthen you in every good deed and word" (steady and strengthen you when you are in trouble) (vv. 16–17). You can count on that! He will give you the strength to do what you need to do, if you choose to do it.

When applied to daily living, this means that believers already have power to do what they ought to do. You *can* put an end to your bad habits. If you are playing around with cocaine, crack, or marijuana, you can stop. You are not bound or limited by those addictions, except as you choose to be; the power of God is ready to help you if you decide to stop. If you are addicted to alcohol or tobacco, you can, by the power of Christ, put an end to those habits. The struggle will not be eliminated altogether, but you will have the strength to keep on fighting day by day until the battle is won.

THE POWER TO CHANGE

Writing from the wicked city of Corinth, Paul asks the Thessalonians to pray for the triumph of the gospel there (3:1 RSV).

God had already wonderfully blessed the apostle's work in Thessalonica, and now he asks the believers there to pray for the Corinthians. God had enabled Paul—in but three short weeks of preaching in the Thessalonian synagogue —to establish a living, vibrant church, calling people out of darkness and the ritual in which they had been bound. Such is the power of the Word of God! Just as that Word spread rapidly among the Thessalonians, revealing its glory and its ability to change people, Paul now prayed that the darkness of Corinth might be similarly dispelled by the light of the gospel.

Many preachers today seem to have lost sight of the naked power of the Word of God. At a recent meeting a pastor told me the story of Dr. Kern, a college professor whom he had met in Germany. This man was a member of the Lutheran Church, the state church of that country. However, he attended church only a couple of times a year, he had never read the Bible, and he had no knowledge of the things of Christ. But because Dr. Kern was a prominent citizen, the church asked him to serve on the board. He agreed and worked diligently. His efforts then resulted in his being asked to serve at the state level, and ultimately on the governing council of the church for the entire nation.

When the professor reached that level, he became convinced that he ought to know something, at least, of the Christian faith. So he took two weeks' vacation and went alone to a quiet retreat where he began to read the Bible. He became so fascinated that he read on and on, sometimes even missing meals, until at the end of the first week he knelt down in his room and cried out to the Lord to save him. The next week he deliberately missed his meals, fasting through the week, and continued to read until he had completed the entire Bible. Dr. Kern returned to his position of leadership a new man and became a catalyst for change in the government of the church. He is now a powerful voice, calling people to reintroduce God and the Scriptures into the dead machinery of the church. That is what the Word of God can do. What a tragedy it is when preachers fail to "hold to" to the teachings of the apostles!

Paul also asked for prayers of protection, "that we may be delivered from wicked and evil men; for not everyone has faith" (v. 2). That last phrase suggests that the opposition he faced was coming from within the church itself. Members who claimed to be believers apparently had no real faith and were making things difficult for Paul. It is interesting to note that he did not ask for the elimination of this opposition but only that he might be delivered through it. God does not often take our trials away. If we ask Him to remove them, He probably will not because He knows our need for trial. What He does promise is that He will take us through the trials. We do not need to fail or give in to wrongful activity, because He has already given us what we need to be overcomers.

Paul closed this part of his letter by assuring the Thessalonian Christians: "The Lord is faithful, and he will strengthen and protect you from the evil one" (v. 3). He knew the Thessalonians well enough to know that by their obedience they would make the choices that would release the power of God. Thus, they could have everything they needed—the love of God and the patience of Christ!

Are you keeping yourself in the love of God? This love will give you a sense of security and worth, a sense of being wanted and needed. It makes no difference what people think about you. "If God is for us, who can be against us?" (Rom. 8:31). Remind yourself frequently of the love of God throughout the day.

He will also give you the patience of Christ—the willingness to wait and watch Him work things out. The Lord never became upset and angry at the resistance He encountered during His earthly ministry. He did not despair through all the terrible trials He had to endure, but "committed himself to him who was able" and waited for Him to work.

That is surely what we need for today. The love of God gives us security, and the patience of Christ gives us consistency. We Christians should be the same day in and day out. We should refuse to become upset and thrown off by circumstances so that we respond like the world around us. Stand firm! And hold to His teachings! God will see us through to the day when we will share the glory of Christ.

IS WORK
A CURSE? 12
(3:6–18)

*I*F YOU HAVE EVER EATEN at any of the Charlie Brown restaurants in California, you will have seen the motto they display: "Work is the curse of the drinking class." This is clearly a reversal of the old maxim: "Drink is the curse of the working class."

Many people think of work as a kind of curse, something that has been imposed upon man because of the Fall. Actually, work is really a blessing, though we tend to forget that at times.

The "flower children" of the sixties got the idea that work was something they did not need and that a good living would somehow fall out of the sky. Many of them dropped out of the rat race, moved out into the countryside, and tried to live without working. Every age has had its freeloaders who want to live off someone else's work. Today it takes the form of those who abuse the welfare system—those who are able to work but will not.

It is interesting that, two thousand years later, we have the same problem as the church in Thessalonica, where certain people refused to work.

Some scholars have argued that these individuals expected the Lord to return at any moment. Here is another strange phenomenon that has assailed the Christian testimony through the centuries.

There is always a lunatic fringe that will push the hope of our Lord's return too far. They use the promise of His coming to develop some kind of far-out activity that brings disrepute upon that doctrine.

Recently I heard of a man who bought a new Cadillac he could not afford. He actually thought he would never have to make another payment because the Lord's return was so imminent!

The apostle Paul does not indicate exactly what was causing this kind of idleness among certain believers in Thessalonica, but he faces the fact of it. It may have been that they were living together in a kind of Christian commune, sharing the labor and the food.

In the book of Acts there is such a reference to the early Christians: "There were no needy persons among them. For from time to time those who owned lands or houses sold them, brought the money from the sales and put it at the apostles' feet, and it was distributed to anyone as he had need" (Acts 4:34–35).

Historians do not feel that this condition existed long in the early church, but it may have been the case in this pioneer church in Thessalonica. At any rate, some people had decided not to work anymore, and they were living off the goodwill and kindness of others. Here Paul addresses the church about them.

THE CURE FOR IDLENESS

Throughout the Scriptures believers are frequently instructed to share with others and to be sensitive to their needs; here, however, Paul issues a stern word regarding "every brother who is idle" (2 Thess. 3:6).

"Keep away" from them, he insists. "Have nothing to do with them. Leave them alone." While this extreme form of ostracism seems unduly painful and even contradictory to other injunctions in the Bible, Paul is on solid theological ground.

1. *A refusal to work is really a violation of Scripture.* Note that this "commandment" bears the imprimatur of the Lord Himself—"in the name of the Lord Jesus Christ" (v. 6). Paul is making no mere suggestion. As Ted Koppel said in his Harvard commencement address: "When Moses came down from the Mount of Sinai he brought the Ten Commandments, not the ten suggestions!" The same is true for these words from Paul. It is a command weighted with the full authority of Jesus Christ.

2. *God ordained work before the fall of man.* When Adam was created he was given a job to do right from the beginning. God commissioned him to name the animals and to till and tend the garden—a beautiful earth filled with wonderful resources, which we have been using up rapidly ever since.

The Lord Himself had said to the disciples: "Put this money to work ... until I come back" (Luke 19:13). Nowhere in His Word does He authorize anyone to stop working *before* His return.

Further, God had declared: "Six days you shall labor and do all your work, but the seventh is a Sabbath to the LORD your God" (Ex. 20:9). Work, then, is part of what the Scriptures call the image of God in man. God is a worker. He has devised marvelous things in a universe that is filled with mysteries and marvels; intricate, involved complexities that we are only now beginning to unravel. With all our modern technological advances, we are merely dabbling in the shallows of the great wonders God has packed into the universe around us, all designed by the working mind of the Creator. Since we are made in the image of God, there are abilities, resources, and possibilities within us that need to be put to work. In so doing we will find fulfillment.

I once saw a bumper sticker that said, "The worst day of fishing is better than the best day of working." If that meant only a day or two of fishing, I could understand the philosophy. Fishing is fun, but I would hate to be sentenced to fishing every day of my life! But I would not mind working, because work is intriguing. It demands something of me; it is worthwhile. Some of you may say, "That may be true for your work, but my work is humdrum and routine. I do the same old things over and over." The Scriptures have a remedy for that problem also: "Whatever you do, whether in word or deed, do all in the name of the Lord Jesus, giving thanks" (Col. 3:17); that is, offer it to Jesus. Even routine work can become palatable if you think of it as a sacrifice to Him; every product you turn out or every pull of the handle can be done as unto the Lord. That is the Christian philosophy of work, by which even humdrum activity can be transformed into that which is meaningful and worthwhile.

3. *Paul set the example for the church to imitate:* "We were not idle when we were with you, nor did we eat anyone's food without paying for it. On the contrary we worked night and day, laboring and toiling" (vv. 7–8).

It is helpful to remember that the great men of God who taught us all these marvelous truths in the Scriptures were not isolated from the ordinary working world but were involved in it. Paul had every right, he said, to stop working. Jesus had said, "The worker deserves his wages" (Luke 10:7); that is, if someone preaches and teaches you spiritual truth, he has the right to expect to be supported in order to give time to his ministry. The apostle recognized this. He said, "Yes, I have that right, but I chose not to do it." Why? "So that we would not be a burden to any of you" (v. 8).

I believe Paul was referring primarily to the establishing of the church. He was a pioneer. He went into places where there were no churches at all, began to preach, and thus brought a local body of believers into being. It was these people, fresh out of paganism, with no recognition in their lives of the value of spiritual truth until they came to Christ, that he wanted to set free from the responsibility to support him. Later on he did receive help from churches. For example, he thanked the Philippians for the help they sent to him in Thessalonica. So it is not true, as some have claimed, that he did not ever receive help or take money from those whom he had led to Christ. Still, because he labored at his trade of tentmaking in order to pay for the food he was eating, it is clear that he deliberately left a model for others in ministry.

During the past months I often thought of Paul as I observed the public humiliation surrounding the moral collapse of a prominent television evangelist. The media covered every move as this man left his multi-million-dollar mansion, boarded his private plane, and flew to a meeting at which he made the vivid confession that all the country has seen. In contrast, I picture the great apostle Paul working by candlelight late into the night, perhaps long after midnight, sewing canvasses together to make tents to sell the next morning so he would have money to pay for the food he was eating. What a contrast! It occurred to me that if this modern-day evangelist had not been so self-indulgent in his life-style, he might have had more spiritual power to resist the temptations to which he succumbed.

A WORD TO BUSYBODIES

Not only were the Thessalonian believers to withdraw socially from Christian brothers who refused to work, but they were actually instructed to withhold food from them.

Notice the distinction, however. It is not, "if any *cannot* work," but, "if any *will not* work." People who cannot work because they are physically impaired or because there is no work to do need our help. Paul is not speaking of legitimate need, but of those con artists who try to invent ways to avoid work.

Hardly a week goes by that we do not have people come to our church offices to ask for financial help. Once a man approached me after the Sunday morning service and asked me to give him some money. He told a heartrending story about how his family was suffering. It was impossible for me to check on whether he was telling the truth or not, so, remembering the words of the Lord in the Sermon on the Mount, "Give to him that asks of you, and do not withhold," I gave him a little money. But I wonder if people like this do not fall into the category Paul is dealing with here. And if we do find out that they can work but do not choose to work, then we should not even give them food. This is what the apostle says.

But Paul was not being hardhearted. His reason for this drastic action—letting people starve if they are able but unwilling to work—was to prevent something worse. People who will not work become busybodies or meddlers, he said, concerning themselves with other people's affairs and stirring up difficulty and trouble. Those who are not busy become busybodies! People who are willing to work are like mules: When they are pulling, they cannot kick; and when they are kicking, they cannot pull!

In verse 12 Paul directly addresses these people: "Such persons we command and urge in the Lord Jesus Christ [again, the authority of Christ] to settle down and earn the bread they eat."

There is no misunderstanding these words. "You can work," says the apostle. "You have an able body and a good mind. Now go to work and earn your own living." Not working when you are able is serious business. Those who refuse to do so are not allowing themselves to be fulfilled in the way God intended. They are cheating others as well, and they are likely to meddle in other people's affairs.

BROTHERS, NOT ENEMIES

The apostle goes on to counsel the leadership of the church on how to handle these problems.

First, do not give up on the idle. They really are brothers. Do not be impatient or "tire" of spending time counseling and encouraging them.

Second, do not evade a confrontation: "Take special note of him." Do not just hope that the problem will pass and do nothing about it. Take note of it.

Third, try to make the idle feel ashamed of themselves. Everyone has a conscience—that little voice inside that protests when we do not fulfill what we were intended to do or be. We may not admit it, but we know inside us when something is wrong. Therefore, Scripture addresses its appeal always to the conscience, to the inner witness that will urge us to do it. Paul's advice is to make freeloaders feel ashamed of their actions, their dependence on others for food and daily necessities.

Finally, do not carry it too far. Do not make these people feel like enemies. Do not make them feel that they are not even Christians. They are confused brothers, and they need help, but they are not unbelievers.

THE IMPORTANCE OF WORK

Why is work so important? What is it about work that the Lord, through the apostle, sees as so valuable that He would take such pains in dealing with it?

Work is divinely intended to give us a sense of self-worth. When we are working, we feel we are accomplishing something. When we are laid off and unable to work, we feel out of sorts and unable to function as we were intended. It is disturbing and psychologically upsetting to be without work, a testimony to the fact that God made us to work. Work, therefore, is not a curse. It is very valuable because it gives a sense of meaning to life.

Lack of work is the explanation for much of the tremendous appeal of drugs to young people. In our large cities crowds of fine young black men and women have nothing to do because they cannot find work. The unemployment level of young blacks today is as high as eighty percent. As a result they turn to that which gives them a temporary feeling of worthwhileness. That is what drugs can do, I am told. How can we blame them for turning to something that at least, if only momentarily, gives them that sense? Of course, in the long run it destroys them. It hooks them so that they cannot get away, and they become slaves to this terrible master.

I am alarmed, frankly, when I see what is happening in our country today. Whole cities are virtually under siege from invading armies of drug traffickers. Authority is being defied on every side. We face a tremendous problem— and often because we have not yet found a solution to the supply of necessary work.

In the thirties, when I was a young man, this country was in the grip of the Great Depression. Thousands of men lost their jobs when businesses were destroyed overnight. There was no work to be found anywhere in those days.

Then the government, under President Franklin D. Roosevelt, came up with a brilliant solution: the Civilian Conservation Corps. Camps, rather like military camps, were built, and there young people, mostly young men, were fed and clothed and given regular work to do. It was simple work. They were paid a minimum amount of money to build reservoirs and dams around the country and to help the farmers with their crops. Several of my friends were saved from a sense of worthlessness by that work program. Perhaps it is time to revive that program again.

GRACE AND PEACE BE WITH YOU

Paul closes this letter to the Thessalonians by recognizing the invisible resources Christians have to deal with any kind of problem. The promise of God is that no matter what our problem, we can have peace in solving it!

So many people who come to me for counsel betray their agitation and anxiety. It is evident in the way they talk and move and act—signs that they are deeply troubled. At times I have had to say: "I will be glad to help you with your problem, but you have another problem that has to be solved first, and that is your lack of peace. You are not peaceful. You are a believer, but you are not at peace, and you will never solve the other problem until you learn how to have peace. The Lord of peace Himself is with you."

When they were caught up in storms on the Sea of Galilee, Jesus said to His disciples: "Take courage! It is I. Don't be afraid" (Matt. 14:27). He was saying: "I am in control. This boat is not going to sink. The Lord of the ocean is in it. Don't be afraid. I am not going to stop the storm, but I will see you through it."

We have the right to take from the Lord of Peace a peaceful mind and heart, and to remind ourselves that He who can handle problems is with us and will help us work this out. Once we are at peace, we can come at the problem with quite a different attitude. This is the way Paul suggests the Thessalonian leaders handle the problem of those who would not work. "The Lord of peace himself give you peace at all times and in every way. The Lord be with all of you" (v. 16).

In closing, as he does in so many of his letters, Paul writes in his own hand. From other letters we learn that the apostle apparently had trouble with poor vision. In his letter to the Galatians he mentions that when he came among them, they would have given him their own eyes had it been possible. Many feel that Paul's thorn in the flesh might have been a visual problem. Thus, when he wrote letters, he usually dictated them to a secretary, one of the men who traveled with him. But at the close of the letter he would take the pen from the hand of the secretary and write these words: "The grace of our Lord Jesus Christ be with you all." A letter bearing this mark was an authentic Pauline epistle.

But it is more than that. It is also evidence that these letters are the very Word of God Himself. The apostle everywhere made claim that the doctrines he taught, the facts he imparted, and the advice and counsel he gave were not his own. They came under inspiration of the Lord— God speaking through a human vessel.

Even in that early day people were counterfeiting the truth. (The Devil is always quick to copy something good.) They were writing letters, supposedly from Paul, and signing his name to them. But when he wrote in his own hand, "The grace of our Lord Jesus Christ be with you all," he imparted an irrefutable proof of authenticity; no one could imitate his signature. When you get a letter like that, said Paul, you know it is written by me. Many liberal scholars reject this second Thessalonian letter as being from Paul because they do not like what it teaches. But here is the mark in this most challenged of his writings—evidence that it is a letter from the apostle himself.

All of this, then, rests upon the grace of our Lord Jesus Christ. The apostle has made his appeal to us to keep working, to work until the Lord comes, to face the problems of life and handle them all with the sense that the Lord of Peace will give us peace in all ways and at all times. What better benediction could we ask!

THE SECOND
COMING OF JESUS

COMMENTATORS HAVE OFTEN portrayed the second coming of Jesus as a single dramatic event (Matt. 24:21, 29), following the Great Tribulation, where the Lord will suddenly appear in power and great glory, visible to every eye (Rev. 1:7). The church will be caught up to meet Him and will then return with Him to earth (1 Thess. 4:13-18) where He will judge the living and dead. This either establishes His millennial kingdom or ushers in the new heaven and new earth, depending on which millennial view the commentator holds.

This scenario has numerous difficulties connected with it, however, not least of which are the several promises in the New Testament that the true church will not be present during the Great Tribulation. A key to understanding the teaching of the New Testament on this subject is the Greek word *parousia*. This word is commonly translated "coming," which in the mind of the reader projects the vision of the single dramatic appearance described above. But *parousia* should properly be translated "presence." This is the meaning given first by both Thayer and Arndt and Gingrich lexicons and includes the idea of an entrance, a consequent duration, and either an exit or a continued presence. It is not, therefore, a single event (V), but a continuum (|_____|) of unspecified duration.

This meaning is the only way to make sense of Jesus' revelation in Matthew 24 of His return to earth in the last days. There He describes a coming in power and glory immediately following the terrible time of trouble that He calls "the great tribulation" and the darkening of the sun and moon and the falling of the stars from heaven (Matt. 24:28–30). But it would be impossible for such a coming to take anyone by surprise who knew of our Lord's description. For in the same chapter Jesus speaks of His coming as unexpected and sudden as the flood came upon the people of Noah's day; and He likens it to a thief creeping into a household at night, without warning, and surreptitiously removing its treasure (vv. 36–44). Yet how could His coming be both unexpected and preceded by such cosmic events of dramatic character?

The only answer is that one passage describes His initial, totally unheralded and unexpected appearing while the other describes the disclosure of His presence by a dramatic display of power and glory after the Tribulation has run its course and the sun, moon, and stars have done their predicted thing.

Jesus' coming like a thief would be a fulfillment of 1 Thessalonians 4:13–18: He would catch up His true church to Himself and then remain on earth during all the events of the Tribulation, but in the same conditions He manifested during His forty-day post-resurrection ministry when He appeared and disappeared at will. After the darkening of the sun and the moon He would disclose His presence to the entire earth in fulfillment of Matthew 24:28–30 and Revelation 1:7. Thus His initial, thieflike coming, His continued presence behind the scenes on earth, and His final revelation in power would all be covered by the term *parousia*. It is noteworthy that where Paul refers to the public revelation of

Jesus in 2 Thessalonians 2:8, he calls it "the splendor of his coming" (NIV), which literally means "the *epiphaneia* ("out-shining") of his *parousia* ("presence").

But what happens to the church after it is caught up to meet the Lord in the air, as 1 Thessalonians 4:13–18 describes? The answer of Scripture is "so shall we ever be with the Lord." Wherever the Lord is, there the church will be also, sharing with Him in His work whatever it will be. But some may object, "I thought the church was to be in heaven with the Lord."

And indeed it will—but what and where is heaven? It is certainly not another place in the cosmos, within the time-space continuum with which we are familiar. In the light of the new physics of Einstein and others, many are coming to see that heaven is a term for another dimension of existence. It need not be spatially removed from us at all, but may be as present on earth as it is anywhere else. When Jesus appeared and disappeared in the course of His post-resurrection ministry, He was simply stepping in and out of the invisible dimension where spiritual realities exist—heaven. Yet all the time He was in some sense on earth, for He said that He had not yet ascended to His Father.

While I admit that this may be somewhat speculative and mysterious, it is supported by several passages of Scripture. It simply implies that the church (consisting of believers with glorified bodies) will accompany the Lord in His behind-the-scenes directing of the events of the Tribulation. It is this same church that the apostle John sees under the symbol of a glorious city, coming from heaven, prepared as a bride adorned for her husband. The marriage supper of the Lamb will already have taken place in those invisible realms while the events of the Tribulation rage on earth.

If anyone wishes to see a further development of these ideas, I have tried to support them with many Scriptures in my book *What's This World Coming To?* published by Regal Books, Ventura, California.

Note to the Reader

The publisher invites you to share your response to the message of this book by writing Discovery House Publishers, Box 3566, Grand Rapids, MI 49501, USA. For information about other Discovery House books, music, or videos, contact us at the same address or call 1-800-653-8333. Find us on the Internet at http://www.dhp.org/ or send E-mail to books@dhp.org.